Winning Shopping Center Designs

Winning Shopping Center Designs

29th International
Design and Development
Awards

 International Council of Shopping Centers

About the International Council of Shopping Centers

This book is based on the information submitted to the International Council of Shopping Centers 29th International Design and Development Awards program. Each shopping center featured in this book was the winner of a Design Award or a Certificate of Merit, as determined by the Awards Committee.

The International Council of Shopping Centers (ICSC) is the trade association of the shopping center industry. Serving the shopping center industry since 1957, ICSC is a not-for-profit organization with more then 54,000 members in 96 countries worldwide.

ICSC members include shopping center

- owners
- developers
- managers
- marketing specialists
- leasing agents
- retailers
- researchers
- attorneys
- architects
- contractors
- consultants
- investors
- lenders and brokers
- academics
- public officials

ICSC holds more then 200 meetings a year throughout the world and provides a wide array of services and products for shopping center professionals, including publications and research data.

For more information about ICSC, please contact:
International Council of Shopping Centers
1221 Avenue of the Americas, 41st Floor
New York, NY 10020-1099
Telephone: (646) 728-3800
Fax: (732) 694-1755
http://www.icsc.org

This publication is designed to provide accurate and authoritative information in regard to the subject matter covered. It is sold with the understanding that the publisher is not engaged in rendering legal, accounting, or other professional services. If legal advice or other expert assistance is required, the services of a competent professional person should be sought.

—From a Declaration of Principles jointly adopted by a Committee of the American Bar Association and a Committee of Publishers.

Published by
INTERNATIONAL COUNCIL OF SHOPPING CENTERS
Publications Department
1221 Avenue of the Americas
New York, NY 10020-1099

BOOK DESIGN: Harish Patel Design, New York, NY

ICSC Catalog Number: 287

International Standard Book Number: 1-58268-065-5

Contents

About the ICSC International Design and Development Awards

The ICSC International Design and Development Awards Program was established to recognize outstanding shopping center projects and to provide information on them to the entire industry so that others may benefit from the experiences of their colleagues.

The 29th International Design and Development Awards Program was worldwide in scope. Participation in other ICSC design awards programs, such as the Canadian or European awards, did not preclude eligible projects from being considered for an International Design and Development Award.

Projects that opened within the 24-month period from July 1, 2002, to June 30, 2004, were eligible for entry into this year's Awards Program.

Awards Categories

Categories for entries were:

Category A—Renovation or Expansion of an Existing Project
Entries had to relate to a project involving an entire shopping center, such as an enclosure, or a single facet of a center, such as an addition. The renovation or expansion must have been completed and the center fully opened for business within the 24-month period from July 1, 2002, to June 30, 2004. Eligible subject matter included, but was not limited to, improving the use of existing space, methods of keeping a center open during construction, new marketing and re-leasing approaches, refinancing techniques, innovative design and construction approaches, and adaptive reuse of the structure.

Category B—Innovative Design and Development of a New Project
Entries had to relate to a specific new shopping center, completed and opened within the 24-month period from July 1, 2002, to June 30, 2004, and must have demonstrated how a specific design or development problem was solved or how new standards in design or development were established. New methods of environmental enhancement, space utilization design themes, energy conservation and innovative construction techniques were among the subjects that were considered for this category. Entries included

detailed information about the design and development of the center, such as explanations of the reasons for, and the realized accomplishments of, the particular approach.

Awards Classifications

Entries submitted for either **category** were judged according to the following center **classification** system:

1. Projects under 150,000 square feet of total retail space*

2. Projects of 150,001 to 500,000 square feet of total retail space*

3. Projects over 500,001 square feet of total retail space.*

*Total retail space includes all square footage included in gross leasable areas (GLA), all department store or other anchor square footage, movie theaters, ice skating rinks, entertainment centers and all peripheral (out-lot) space engaged in retail enterprise. It does not include office or hotel square footage.

Eligibility

1. The ICSC International Design and Development Awards Program was open only to ICSC member companies. Any ICSC member company could enter as many projects as desired in either of the two categories.

2. Entries must have had the authorization and signature of the owner or management company of the property.

3. Projects opened within the 24-month period from July 1, 2002, to June 30, 2004, were eligible.

4. Projects must have been completed and opened for business by June 30, 2004.

5. Separate phases of a project could be submitted individually, provided they were completed and opened for business by June 30, 2004.

6. Projects could only be submitted once. Projects that were entered in the past could not be resubmitted unless substantial changes were made since the last submission.

7. Members entering the ICSC Canadian or ICSC European awards programs had to submit separately to the International Design and Development Awards Program, and entries had to adhere to its entry guidelines and requirements. Entries accepted into other ICSC awards programs did not automatically qualify for this program, nor was any entry excluded simply because it was an award winner in another program.

If you have any questions about the International Council of Shopping Centers International Design and Development Awards, or would like to receive an application for the upcoming awards program, please contact:

International Council of Shopping Centers
International Design and Development Awards
1221 Avenue of the Americas
41st Floor
New York, NY 10020-1099
(646) 728-3462
www.icsc.org

Foreword

This year's entries to the 29th ICSC International Design and Development Awards established a record international presence, as 46% of this year's 39 entries came from 16 countries outside of the United States.

There were 21 finalists in the category of "Innovative Design and Development of a New Project," with developers, architects and investors exhibiting very creative solutions in some of the more mature markets. And, in the category of "Renovation or Expansion of an Existing Project," there were nine finalists.

A high level of excellence was reflected in this year's 6 Award winners and 15 Certificate of Merit recipients, and their efforts played a vital role in the continued growth and success within the shopping center industry.

In addition to the trend of creating progressive mixed-use developments, we also found many winning projects in strong markets recognizing the need to revitalize their centers to meet changing market expectations, such as SouthPark Mall, United States; Shopping Center Iguatami Fortaleza, Brazil; Mall Plaza Norte, Chile; Namba Parks, Japan; and Kamp-Promenade, Germany. A few projects applied unconventional approaches by successfully converting breweries, bullrings or railroad stations into bustling retail-oriented mixed-use venues. Some projects to note include Stary Browar, Poland; Bullring, United Kingdom; and Estação, Portugal.

The International Design and Development Awards Jury Committee is composed of 12 industry leaders from development, retailing, architecture, financial investment and consulting firms, averaging in excess of 25 years' experience each. Committee members devoted many hours to judging this year's submissions. In addition to fine-tuning the online submission process and revamping the awards presentation ceremony at the CenterBuild Conference in December 2005. Both improvments were met with overwhelming approval, and I am very grateful to the committee for its dedication and professionalism.

Most of all, this book honors the winning submissions in this year's International Design and Development Awards. We thank the entrants for their creativity, resourcefulness and hard work. We hope this recognition inspires future projects to provide world-class shopping and entertainment experiences.

Rao K. Sunku
JCPenney Company

Chairman
ICSC 2005 International Design and Development Awards
Jury Committee

Acknowledgments

The International Council of Shopping Centers 29th International Design and Development Awards were selected by a committee of diverse shopping center professionals representing retailers, developers and architects. The International Council of Shopping Centers is grateful to these judges for the time, effort and expertise they contributed to the awards program.

Rao K. Sunku, *Chairman*
JCPenney Company
Dallas, Texas

Ronald A. Altoon, FAIA
Altoon + Porter Architects
Los Angeles, California

Tom Brudzinski
General Growth Properties, Inc.
Columbia, Maryland

F. Carl Dieterle, Jr.
Simon Property Group
Indianapolis, Indiana

Arcadio Gil Pujol, ASM
LaSBA, S.A.
Madrid, Spain

Gordon T. Greeby
The Greeby Companies, Inc.
Lake Bluff, Illinois

Daryl Mangan
Retail Properties Solutions, LLC
Vestavia Hills, Alabama

John M. Millar, SCSM
Divaris Real Estate, Inc.
Virginia Beach, Virginia

Kathleen Nelson
KMN Associates, Inc.
East Atlantic Beach, New York

J. Thomas Porter
Thompson, Ventulett, Stainback & Associates
Atlanta, Georgia

Ian F. Thomas
Thomas Consultants, Inc.
Vancouver, BC, Canada

Gerald M. White
Copaken, White & Blitt
Leawood, Kansas

Bullring
Birmingham, United Kingdom

Owner and Management Company:
The Birmingham Alliance
Birmingham, United Kingdom

Design Architect:
Benoy
London, United Kingdom

Production Architect:
Chapman Taylor
London, United Kingdom

Landscape Architect:
Gross Max
Edinburgh, United Kingdom

General Contractor:
Sir Robert McAlpine
Birmingham, United Kingdom

Development Company:
The Birmingham Alliance
Birmingham, United Kingdom

Leasing Companies:
Cushman & Wakefield Healey & Baker
London, United Kingdom
Jones Lang LaSalle
Birmingham, United Kingdom
Lunson Mitchenall
London, United Kingdom

Gross size of center:
1,183,600

Gross leasable area (small shop space, excluding anchors):
1,158,640 sq. ft.

Total acreage of site:
26 acres

Type of center:
Regional

Physical description:
Three-level open-air and enclosed mall

Location of trading area:
Urban Business District

Population:
- Primary trading area
  4.2 million

- Secondary trading area
  7.2 million

Development schedule:
- Opening date
  September 4, 2003

Parking spaces:
- 3,100

St. Martin's Church received a high-tech backdrop with the construction of Bullring in Birmingham.

Photograph: Michael Betts

*T*hrough a strong partnership between public and private interests, the three-level Bullring has revitalized retailing in downtown Birmingham, England.

The former Bull Ring shopping center, built in the 1960's, had grown dull and dated. The Birmingham Alliance, a private partnership, worked closely with the Birmingham City Council in all development phases of the new Bullring, particularly on transportation issues.

Erasing the old Bull Ring involved removal of 72,000 tons of concrete and 13,000 tons of steelwork, as well as 2.2 million square feet of excavation. Most materials were recycled in other projects. The new Bullring would use over one million concrete blocks, 969,000 square feet of concrete and 17,000 tons of structural steelwork (twice

Photograph: Hufton & Crowe 2003

Photograph: Hufton & Crowe 2003

Photograph: Michael Betts

Aerial views of the old Bull Ring (top) and the new mall (center) show how today's design fits in with existing city streets. St. Martin's Church sits in the center of the project. The futuristic look of the Bullring exterior is an eye-catcher for pedestrians (right).

the weight of the Eiffel Tower).

Bullring draws on the historic downtown street patterns in its mix of traditional streets, squares and open spaces. Existing landmarks – the old Moor Street train station and St. Martin's Church – have been cleaned and restored. Long-lost Birmingham street names, some from the 18th century, have been reintroduced.

The center comprises several city blocks, each with its own proportions and styles, and each connecting seamlessly with the existing city center. The church, in particular, is in a public square, giving it an identity independent of Bullring.

Bullring's development included revitalization of Moor Street's Edwardian train station, whose ticket office was reopened after 16 years of nonuse. Existing rail lines and other forms of mass transit bring 60 percent of Bullring's visitors. Plans call for restoration of some older train platforms in 2007-2008.

Construction presented many challenges. The busy city center location held two railway stations and two bus terminals. Public access had to be maintained across both the north and south sides of the site, requiring a temporary pedestrian bridge 750 feet long.

Inside, a 75,000-square-foot "sky-plane" roof provides a virtually invisible glass cover over Bullring's seemingly open malls,

Photograph: Hufton & Crowe 2003

Photograph: Michael Betts

Plazas like this (top) link the center to city streets. Three graceful wands (right) are among the $3.6 million in artwork on permanent display at Bullring.

giving the impression of a natural extension of the city's key shopping streets while linking them to the two department stores. Rather than joining the facades symmetrically, as is often found in traditional shopping mall design, the roof allows all the blocks and areas to take on different architectural treatments.

The visual consistency with nearby streets is reinforced by use of stone, metal, brick and glass storefronts in the center, which bring an outdoor feeling to the enclosed mall spaces. The roof also allows traffic year-round, despite England's cold winters.

The enormous glazed "sky-plane" roof brings the outside in over Gap (above). Debenham's department store (bottom) is clearly marked at all three shopping levels.

Photograph: Hufton & Crowe 2003

Photograph: Hufton & Crowe 2003

A signage pylon (above) and a three-level, multiwing atrium (right). The mall exterior (below) blends in with city streets.

Photograph: Michael Betts

Two buildings on Bullring's northern perimeter were suspended from four massive 132-ton, 164-foot street trusses, accommodating existing roads and fragile Victorian-era railway tunnels below. These trusses form a dramatic gateway to Bullring and give scale and presence to the street junction at the base of Bullring's Rotunda. They also link Bullring to existing downtown retailing.

The developers spent $3.6 million on artwork to enhance the mall's public realms. Commissioned artwork includes three graceful wands, a collection of boldly illuminated glass blocks and a bronze bull, which has become widely recognized as the mall's icon.

Bullring is anchored by two department stores, Selfridges and Debenhams. The mall also offers 146 shops, cafes and restaurants. The retail mix is mid- to upscale,

MAJOR TENANTS		
NAME	**TYPE**	**GLA (SQ. FT.)**
Selfridges	Department store	255,900
Debenhams	Department store	204,700

Photograph: Ravi Deepres

Retailers (left) benefit from personalized, discreet signage. The bold visual scale even extends to vertical transport (below) via escalators.

Photograph: Ravi Deepres

with TK Maxx, Virgin Megastore, Goldsmiths and Louis Vuitton among them. Some retailers already represented in the city took second or third outlets in the mall.

Developers founded Bullring Jobs 2003, a joint recruitment campaign with the city, to attract job seekers for Bullring's 8,000 new employment opportunities. Partners included the City Council, The Birmingham Alliance, the local learning and skills council and other job-focused entities. Of the new jobs available, 70 percent were filled through the Bullring Jobs program. Of those, 76 percent were taken by people who had been unemployed and over 50 percent by people from key priority wards of the city.

Bullring's opening attracted over one million people in the first four days. Over 10 million customers visited in the first three months. The sales success is shown in the 2004 UK Experian Retail Ranking report, which raised Birmingham from the15th-ranked United Kingdom retail site to 3rd, as a result of Bullring's presence.

Photograph: Ravi Deepres

Lively street entertainment (top) and a stunning evening presence (below) show how Bullring has successfully revitalized downtown Birmingham.

Photograph: Hufton & Crowe 2003

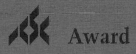

Estação Viana
Viana do Castelo, Portugal

Owner and Management Company:
Sonae Sierra
Maia, Portugal

Design Architect:
Laguarda.Low Architects
Dallas, Texas, United States

Production Architect:
Cabeza & Sastre
Lisbon, Portugal

Graphic Designer:
Redmond Schwartz Mark Design
Los Angeles, California, United States

Lighting Designer:
T. Kondos & Associates
New York, New York, United States

Landscape Architect:
Hipólito Bettencourt
Lisbon, Portugal

General Contractors:
Engil
Lisbon, Portugal
PréGaia
Porto, Portugal
Martifer
Oliveira de Frades, Portugal

Development Companies:
Sonae Sierra
Maia, Portugal
Estação Shopping
Viana do Castelo, Portugal

Leasing Companies:
Sonae Sierra
Maia, Portugal
C&W H&B
Lisbon, Portugal

Gross size of center:
628,273 sq. ft.

Gross leasable area (small shop space, excluding anchors):
199,758 sq. ft.

Total acreage of site:
4.22 acres

Type of center:
Regional

Physical description:
Five-level enclosed mall

Location of trading area:
City Center

Population:
• Primary trading area
  36,600

• Secondary trading area
  133,700

Development schedule:
• Opening date
  November 19, 2003

Parking spaces:
• 600

The railroad tracks that run under Estação Viana in Portugal inspired design highlights in the center itself.

*E*stação Viana (Viana Station)
draws its design concept from an
adjacent railway station in Viana
do Castelo, a port city in northern
Portugal bounded by mountains,
the Atlantic Ocean and the Lima
River.

At its city-center location,
Estação Viana literally sits atop
train tracks. Designers sought to
absorb the station's history,
shapes, sounds, smells and experiences in creating the new center.

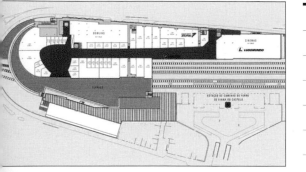

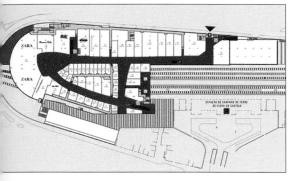

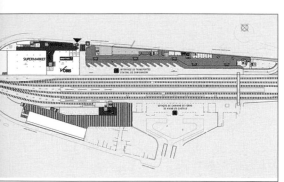

The ground floor (lowest illustration) shows the train tracks, part of the public transport exchange for trains, buses and taxis, which is run by the city.

MAJOR TENANTS		
NAME	TYPE	GLA (SQ. FT.)
Supermarcado da Estação	Supermarket	22,142
Zara	Clothing	15,737
Castello Lopes	Cinemas	15,403
BUGZ	Bowling and leisure	12,701
Worten / Vobis	Electronic appliances	9,192
Sportzone	Sports	7,782
Modalfa	Clothing	4,316

The long, lean lines of the center (right) reinforce the train-themed design. At night, Estação Viana's brightly lit exterior invites shoppers.

Shelters, graphic panels, the logo and other design elements all reflect the theme of trains. An overhead miniature train circles the food court and leisure plaza. Even the shape of the center – long and slender – hints at the train tracks below.

Because of its location, Estação Viana serves as a bridge between the city's older and newer sections. The city's public transport exchange for trains, buses and taxis is on the center's ground floor. The operating railway lines, however, presented problems during the development, so the trains ran on a tighter schedule during the construction period.

There are five levels in the center, two for parking and three offering retail, a food court, cinemas and leisure-time activity. A 6,500-square-foot cultural space near the development's south entrance is accessible to residents of both sections and has helped revitalize the city center. The community is also served by the food court and

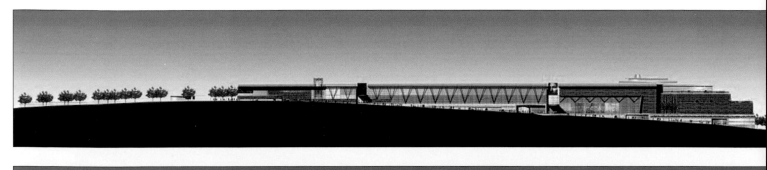

A circular entryway (above) beckons shoppers and community alike into the food court at night, while polished floors, glass and bright lights (left) make an attractive backdrop for retail stores.

supermarket and by services such as a children's playground, diaper-changing rooms, children's rest-rooms and an infrastructure designed to aid people with dis-abilities.

International retail brands such as Stradivarius, Pull & Bear and Massimo Dutti sit alongside well-known local shops. There are 7 anchors, 16 restaurants and 87 small shops. At opening, 99 per-cent of the center's gross leasable area was committed. As a policy, 20 percent of the shops are leased to local tenants, including such brands as Bodegão restaurant and fashion shops Salto Raso and Kids' Blue. In all, nearly one-half of all shops offer clothing and about one-fifth are devoted to food, including the food court.

Windows (top and bottom) tie Estação Viana to the com-munity, from inside and out.

The center uses current technology, including digital closed-circuit televisions, low-consumption lamps, foot-fall and car-counting systems and television monitors in the restrooms. Glass is used extensively throughout the facility. Floors combine stone, ceramic materials and terrazzo. Exteriors include decorative concrete pre-cast panels, stone, ceramic tiles, metallic panels and glass.

In its ongoing tribute to the world of the railroad, Estação Viana has also become an engine for retail growth and community life in Viana do Castelo.

The warm sun of Portugal is reflected in the design of the flooring (above). There are five levels, including a food court (below).

Shoppers, tourists and visitors (below) comprise busy crowds at the area's only major mall.

Plantings, the glass roof and tiled floor accents offer visual appeal to the shopping experience of Estação Viana (above and below).

Kamp-Promenade

Osnabrück, Germany

Owner:
WestInvest Gesellschaft für Investmentfonds mbH
Düsseldorf , Germany

Management Company:
Multi Mall Management Germany GmbH
Düsseldorf, Germany

Design Architect:
T+T Design
Gouda, The Netherlands

Production Architect:
Lindemann und Partner
Bràunschweig, Germany

Lighting Designer:
Conceptlicht
Mills, Austria

Landscape Architect:
WES Wehberg, Eppinger, Schmidtke
Hamburg, Germany

General Contractor:
Hochtief Construction AG
Osnabrück, Germany

Development Company:
Multi Development Germany GmbH
Düsseldorf, Germany

Gross size of center:
169,318 sq. ft.

Gross leasable area (small shop space, excluding anchors):
169,318 sq. ft.

Total acreage of site:
1.56 acres

Type of center:
Regional mixed-use

Physical description:
Open-air and office buildings

Location of trading area:
Urban

Population:
- Primary trading area
  167,000

- Secondary trading area
  750,000

Development schedule:
- Opening date
  June 2004

Parking spaces:
- 250

*K*amp-Promenade shopping center is a multipurpose retail center in downtown Osnabrück, Germany. The center has created a small new district for the city, consisting of several distinctive buildings on a site that had been underused since World War II, most recently as a parking lot.

Unlike many city-center shopping centers, Kamp-Promenade has no covered mall but is instead a public area within a private property,

Trapezoidal and triangular building shapes are among the unique design elements of Germany's Kamp-Promenade.

MAJOR TENANTS		
NAME	TYPE	GLA (SQ. FT.)
Saturn	——	48,438
Karstadt Sport	——	26,910
Esprit	Clothing	11,840
Kult Company	——	11,302

Computer renderings (left top and center) are borne out with great accuracy at the real Kamp-Promenade (below left).

Wide-open storefronts attract shoppers (right).

restoring a part of the original city center.

Retail, including restaurants and food courts, makes up most of the center. About 17 percent of the space is given to offices. There is an underground garage.

The proximity of the project to city streets presented major problems, since there was no significant space available for setting up the construction site. To build the garage, the groundwater table had to be lowered without damaging surrounding developments and vegetation – and local residents could not have their water-supply and waste routes disturbed. Careful planning of space, schedule and sequence made the project physically feasible.

Kamp-Promenade brings new shoppers to the Osnabrück city center (left and below).

Kamp-Promenade's designers felt it was important that the facades use distinctive colors and carefully selected materials to create a striking piece of architecture that would form a perfect link between the old town of Osnabrück and this supermodern retail structure.

The four buildings are all completely different in terms of height, color and shape (triangle, trapezoid, passageway and pavilion). The roofs were designed to give them an attractive fifth facade when viewed from above or from the upper stories of nearby buildings. Visible heating systems were carefully positioned, then enclosed behind facades to conceal them. The remaining roof

The designers felt it was important that the facades use distinctive colors and carefully selected materials to create a striking piece of architecture (above and below).

areas were largely covered with vegetation or with terrace flooring.

The unusual architecture complements the high degree of functionality of Kamp-Promenade and its open structure adds style to Osnabrück's city center. There is now another top address for retailers and offices. Neighboring property owners have also modernized their properties – an indication of the center's power as a city landmark.

The key to the project, the developers say, is the meticulous way in which Kamp-Promenade has been integrated into the existing structure of the city and how existing pedestrian routes and visual paths have been merged into the property. The view to the tower of nearby St. Katherine's Church, for example, was opened in a striking manner, and residents have a new view of the city skyline through the center's passageway.

Overall, Kamp-Promenade demonstrates the value of customizing design and development plans to a specific site rather than relying on standard formulas. Even more expensive solutions to some problems – the underground garage, for example, or the multibuilding format – will add to the long-range value of Kamp-Promenade.

Shoppers, nearby residents and office workers are all attracted to Kamp-Promenade.

Visitors to Kamp-
Promenade can enjoy
food and beverages
(above) and shop
(below left), with the
option of parking in
the underground
garage (below right).

Mall Plaza Norte
Santiago, RM, Chile

Owner and Management Company:
Plaza Oeste S. A. (Mall Plaza)
Santiago, RM, Chile

Design Architect:
TVS International
Atlanta, Georgia, United States

Production Architect:
Jaime Vargas C.
Santiago, RM, Chile

Graphic Designer:
Proyectos Corporativos
Santiago, RM, Chile

Lighting Designer:
PBS Arquitectos
Santiago, RM, Chile

Landscape Architect:
Arnello & Viveros Arquitectos
Santiago, RM, Chile

General Contractor:
Salfacorp.
Santiago, RM, Chile

Development and Leasing Company:
Mall Plaza
Santiago, RM, Chile

Gross size of center:
1,829,865 sq. ft.

Gross leasable area (small shop space, excluding anchors):
283,000 sq. ft.

Total acreage of site:
39.5 acres

Type of center:
Regional power

Physical description:
Two-level enclosed mall

Location of trading area:
Suburban

Population:
- Primary trading area
  516,864
- Annualized percentage of shoppers anticipated to be from outside trade area
  26.1%

Development schedule:
- Opening date
  November 27, 2003

Parking spaces:
- 2,284

Extensive use of glass allows the bright Chilean sunshine into Mall Plaza Norte in Santiago.

*M*all Plaza Norte is a new mixed-use center in Santiago, Chile's capital and largest city. Medical offices coexist with retail and big-box stores are close to performing arts venues.

The center opened on November 27, 2003. It has three main department stores, one home-center superstore, an auto-service center, 120 small stores and restaurants, along with two office towers. Parking, available above and below grade, is connected to the center via escalators and stairs.

Local consumers had high expectations for the project. Previously, nearby residents would have to travel great distances to find commercial, cultural and entertainment facilities. Now, the blend of retail, entertainment and food/beverage has made Mall Plaza Norte into the place of encounter for the surrounding communities.

The center's design embraces the natural beauty of the surrounding mountains, offering many scenic views. The center uses glass exteriors extensively, bringing in natural light to enliven the interiors.

An outdoor entertainment plaza – placed to take advantage of the sunny mountain views and a future subway station – creates a

A crescent configuration (above) allows maximum visibility of all the mall's components despite limited frontage on the main highway.

social gathering destination for the community. The entertainment plaza includes a performing arts theater, a library and a branch of the national art museum.

Several site issues emerged during the development process. The site is small and irregularly shaped, which conflicted with the physical size demands of the project's elements and parking needs. Further, the site is flanked on both sides by factory and warehouse buildings. It has limited frontage along the main roadway and narrow views between the existing industrial buildings.

These issues were resolved by arranging the buildings into a shallow crescent configuration that gives maximum roadway visibility to all major uses. Most parking was moved below grade. The mall entrance was given a

Sweeping interplay of glass with curved walls and ceilings give a futuristic look to the mall inside and out.

sweeping, dramatic all-glass presence, turning it into a visual icon for the project.

The glass-entrance atrium serves as the arrival court for customers from both above and underground parking. It also creates the mall's central gathering space and connects the open-air entertainment area with the enclosed fashion mall.

Visually, the center has many bold touches, befitting its new role as a community center and giving it an identity despite the overwhelming presence of the mountains nearby. Some building edifices are wide expanses of clear glass. Ceilings are dotted with glass inserts at many locations. The color scheme emphasizes off-white shades to enhance the natural sunlight that enters through window walls and atria. Limited use of brick and wood offers accent points. Undulating backlights in some

Retail, office space, restaurants and cultural amenities all find a home in the varied shapes and textures (left) of Mall Plaza Norte.

Natural light (right and below) creates an ever-changing visual geometry within the center.

MAJOR TENANTS

NAME	TYPE	GLA (SQ. FT.)
Lider	Hypermarket	168,175
Homecenter	Superstore	125,776
Integramedica	Medical center	77,123
Falabella	Department store	72,915
Paris	Department store	72,915
Ripley	Department store	66,521
Autoplaza	Car showroom/service	52,765
Cinemark	Multiscreen theater	33,433

Movie theaters, the national art museum, food courts and the entry plaza (left) work together to create a true community gathering spot for Santiago's citizens and tourists. An innovative ceiling above the food court suggests movement (right). Plenty of convenient parking (below) encourages regular visits.

ceilings suggest movement above the large food court. There are several art installations, including a fountain where sculptures of three cherubs are depicted splashing happily.

The developers believe that Mall Plaza Norte's success at integrating retail and entertainment sets a new standard for Chile's shopping centers.

Mall Plaza Norte has many bold touches, including public sculptures and design accents (above and right).

Stary Browar

Poznań, Poland

Owner and Management Company:
Fortis Sp. z o.o.
Poznań, Poland

Design and Production Architect:
Studio ADS Sp. z o.o.
Poznań, Poland

Graphic Designers:
Ryszard Kaja
Poznań, Poland
Studio ADS Sp. z o.o.
Poznań, Poland

Lighting Designer:
Studio ADS Sp. z o.o.
Poznań, Poland

Landscape Architect:
Studio ADS Sp. z o.o.
Poznań, Poland

General Contractor:
PORR Projekt und Hochbau AG
Absberggasse, Vienna, Austria

Development and Leasing Company:
Fortis Sp. z o.o.
Poznań, Poland

Gross size of center:
699,654 sq. ft.

Gross leasable area (small shop space, excluding anchors):
326,146 sq. ft.

Total acreage of site:
18.2 acres

Type of center:
Mixed-use

Physical description:
Four-level open-air and enclosed mall

Location of trading area:
Downtown

Population:
- Primary trading area
  227,400
- Secondary trading area
  351,500
- Annualized percentage of shoppers anticipated to be from outside trade area
  22%

Development schedule:
- Opening date
  November 6, 2003

Parking spaces:
- 400

Stary Browar center in western Poland is an old brewery site that has been converted into retail, entertainment, food and office uses.

*T*ake a 19th-century brewery, add new retail, office, food and entertainment uses, and there is Stary Browar, the new shopping, art and business center in the heart of the city of Poznań in western Poland.

The project, completed within 18 months, involved 27 contractors. Now there are 97 stores, a seven-unit food court, a 71,000-square-foot entertainment/leisure center and nearly 54,000 square feet of office space on the center's four levels.

MAJOR TENANTS		
NAME	**TYPE**	**GLA (SQ. FT.)**
MegaAvans	Multimedia	32,776
Piotr I Pawel	Supermarket	30,537
H&M	Clothes	21,216
Zara	Clothes	15,102
Smyk	Children's clothes and toys	13,939
Cubus	Children's clothes	10,527
Royal Collection	Clothes	9,666
Reserved	Casual clothes	7,664

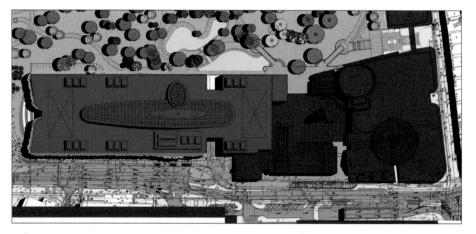

Architect's renderings show the large scale of the Stary Browar project. In the plot plan (left), the brewery site is at right, connected to the new retail area by a courtyard.

The mall's sections are separate but well-integrated. The eastern section is the commercial center; the southern leads to office space; and the northern side borders the park.

Stary Browar benefits from a good location, despite the presence of five shopping centers in 12 miles and another four planned to open soon. Stary Browar sits at the center of a dense network of public roads — actually on Pólwiejska Street, a popular shopping venue. The center's main access road is a national and international thoroughfare. The mall is less than 100 feet from a tram stop. The main country railway and coach

The red brick, glass and metal of the brewery design are reflected in the new mall's exteriors.

The industrial look — often avoided in modern center design — works well for modern retailing at Stary Browar.

stations are less than a 10-minute walk away. The historical heart of the city — Old Market Square — is a six-minute walk, and the center is only 20 minutes from the airport. An adjacent park is owned by the developer and provides a green area next to the center's leisure sector.

The deteriorating Huggar Brothers brewery, built in 1876, served that function until the 1980's. In the 1990's, it held a soft-drink production company. The complex contained a six-level malt house, boiler house, storage cellar and villa, which were all given new functions and treated with respect during the construction of Stary Browar center. Some buildings were demolished in the past decade. The new buildings were

Public uses are built into the functionality of Stary Browar. A large sculpture and seating areas show the developer's intent to offer more than shopping.

Nearly a dozen food locations (above and below) can be found at Stary Browar.

to be considered architectural extensions of the rehabilitated exteriors of the old brewery. Red brick, glass and metal create the exterior look of both the old brewery and new mall. Paving stones, wood, metal and granite are used in the floors.

The old malt house and a new three-story gallery host artistic and photographic exhibitions, presenting contemporary designers, theatrical performances, modern choreography and cinema. There is also a 35,000-square-foot art courtyard for public use. Local artists are featured there when possible.

Stary Browar's developers anticipate future growth. A second retail phase will be built to the center's west, connected to the current center by an internal piazza. The art courtyard will be covered by a roof. Six hundred parking spaces will be added to the current 400.

The center created over 1,000 new jobs for Poznańs residents. It has sparked a more general development of downtown Poznań by offering the city a new image and renewed determination over its economic future by literally building on its past.

Sensible guidelines for storefronts gave creative structure to the designers' imagination.

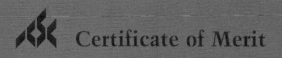

Klanderij

Enschede, The Netherlands

Owner:
Fortis Vastgoed B.V.
Utrecht, The Netherlands

Management Company:
WPM Winkelcentrummanagement B.V.
Amsterdam, The Netherlands

Architects:
De Architekten Cie
Amsterdam, The Netherlands
The Jerde Partnership International Inc.
Venice, California, United States

Lighting Designer:
Art Concept Technology
St.-Pieters-Leeuw, Belgium

Landscape Architect:
West 8
Rotterdam, The Netherlands

General Contractor:
Heijmans IBC Bouw Arnhem B.V.
Arnhem, The Netherlands

Development Companies:
Foruminvest B.V.
Naarden, The Netherlands
Prowinko Nederland B.V.
Amsterdam, The Netherlands

Leasing Company:
Jos Dobbe Makelaardij B.V.
Noordwijk, The Netherlands

Gross size of center:
258,336 sq. ft.

Gross leasable area (small shop space, excluding anchors):
219,586 sq. ft.

Total acreage of site:
4.45 acres

Type of center:
Regional

Physical description:
Open-air and enclosed mall

Center's trade area:
Center city

Population:
• Primary trading area
  150,000

• Secondary trading area
  350,000

• Annualized percentage of shoppers anticipated to be from outside trade area
  20%

Development schedule:
• Opening date
  October 30, 2003

Parking spaces:
• 1,700

*K*landerij, a new shopping center in Enschede, the Netherlands, sits on the site of an old center (Klanderij Passade). The city, located 10 miles west of the German border, had once been the center of Holland's textile industry. It had been losing retail sales for years to such nearby cities as Hengelo and Oldenzaal and the German cities of Nordhorn and Gronau.

The center, partially open and partially enclosed, is located in the city center on the largest market square in the eastern part of the Netherlands. It lies next to department stores C&A, V&D and Bijenkorf. Shoppers can approach Klanderij from the city's main pedestrian street. They can also use the 1,700 parking spaces and 1,050 cycle sheds at the center. A national airport lies four miles away.

Klanderij uses warmly colored natural finishings throughout its interior design. Special attention was paid to lighting, designed by experts who had worked for entertainment icons Celine Dion and Cirque du Soleil. The concept was to remind people of their living rooms at home, down to the choice of lampshades. Likewise, materials for the ceiling — copper and wood — were selected for their home-like appearance.

High-quality materials were used throughout the center. The developer imported Oregon pine wooden beams and used 26 types of

Photograph: Copyright AVEQ Fotografie – & AV Producties

A bold sculpture welcomes shoppers to Klanderij in the eastern section of the Netherlands, near the German border.

marble, along with mosaic stones. Many types of stone were brought from India and the United States and are used inside to give shoppers the sense of walking in an outdoor environment.

Inside, the center is a bold mix of wide, open storefronts. Each shop was able to come up with its own storefront design within parameters set by the developer and mall designer. Special signboards permit individual shopowners to insert their own photographs.

Each shop was responsible for its own climate-control installations.

The center's air supply is ventilated naturally by windows in the roof of the passageways and Klanderij's main square.

Armed with the center's design, the developers were able to attract international retailers to fill half of the center's stores, which they felt was an important step in bringing shoppers to the mall. There was a particular challenge here, in that the international retailers had previously been drawn only to Holland's four largest cities (Enschede is the 10th largest).

The high ceiling (left) contrasts nicely with the street-scale storefronts, giving shoppers a sense of simultaneous spaciousness and intimacy.

Special lighting fixtures (below) were chosen to make the open mall area feel like someone's living room.

Photograph: Copyright AVEQ Fotografie – & AV Producties

Photograph: Copyright AVEQ Fotografie – & AV Producties

Klanderij's designers were careful to include public amenities. An exhibition gallery offers the local university the opportunity to display projects every four months. Together with generous interior landscaping and lanterns in the covered square, Klanderij provides a pleasant ambience for shopping.

Natural light (right and below) streams through ceiling windows, which can be opened for ventilation. Wide storefronts (bottom) give top priority to merchandise at the stores of Klanderij.

Photograph: Copyright AVEQ Fotografie – & AV Producties

Photograph: Copyright AVEQ Fotografie – & AV Producties

MAJOR TENANTS

NAME	TYPE	GLA (SQ. FT.)
Media Markt	Electronics	53,303
Hennes & Mauritz	Clothing	24,391
Miss Etam	Women's fashion	16,157

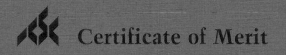
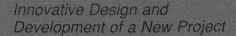
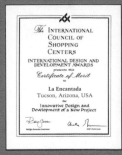

La Encantada

Tucson, Arizona, United States

Owner and Management Company:
Westcor Partners
Phoenix, Arizona, United States

Design Architect:
Callison Architecture, Inc.
Seattle, Washington, United States

Production Architect:
Burlini/Silberschlag
Tucson, Arizona, United States

Graphic Designer:
Callison Architecture, Inc.
Seattle, Washington, United States

Lighting Designer:
Candela
Seattle, Washington, United States

Landscape Architect:
TMHS Associates
Tucson, Arizona, United States

General Contractor:
T.L. Roof & Associates
Tucson, Arizona, United States

Development and Leasing Company:
Westcor Partners
Phoenix, Arizona, United States

Gross size of center:
269,468 sq. ft.

Gross leasable area (small shop space, excluding anchors):
258,000 sq. ft.

Total acreage of site:
36.7 acres

Type of center:
Lifestyle

Physical description:
Open-air

Center's trade area:
Suburban

Population:
- Primary trading area
  478,500

- Secondary trading area
  800,000

- Annualized percentage of shoppers anticipated to be from outside trade area
  35%

Development schedule:
- Opening date
  March 2004

Parking spaces:
- 1,600

Designers of La Encantada in Tucson, Arizona, based their design palette on the muted tones of the surrounding desert.

*L*a Encantada in sunny Tucson, Arizona, both respects and benefits from its pleasant surroundings.

Sensitivity to the natural environment was paramount among the design priorities of the two-level open air center. Much of the site planning and building design centered on ways to touch the land lightly and take advantage of the center's dramatic mountain and desert views.

Design follows the contours of the sloping site, rather than leveling it

The center capitalizes on a natural drainage site as a landscape feature and incorporates native vegetation, rock outcroppings and water throughout the project. Even the parking lot contains clusters of local sweet acadia and mesquite trees. Further, the developer left eight acres undisturbed, to preserve the site's beauty as well as its wildlife, which was relocated during construction.

Tucson's residents pride themselves on their unique community, and designers sought to bring

before construction. This allows shoppers to enjoy a variety of excellent views of the mountains and valley as they wander up and down La Encantada's walkways.

Traditional hot-climate design elements have been used, such as thick walls, interior courtyards with water features, arcades, canopies and large roof overhangs. These allow the center the benefits of winter sunlight and shelter from the intense desert heat of the summer.

The center's two levels (above) provide plenty of public space.

Wrought iron, timber and tile (below) reflect the building materials abundant in local design.

MAJOR TENANTS

NAME	TYPE	GLA (SQ. FT.)
Al's	Specialty foods	29,316
Crate&Barrel	Home	16,817
Anthropologie	Fashion, home, accessories	10,430
Talbots	Fashion	6,016
Tommy Bahama	Resortwear	4,200
Apple	Computers	3,800

that sense to La Encantada. Inspired by the work of local designer Josias Joseler, the architects worked with — rather than against — the desert. Visitors approach the main arrival area at the lower end of the complex and wind their way through courtyards, breezeways and patios ringed by shops. They can proceed to an upper promenade and restaurant plaza that features a fireplace, often welcomed on cool summer nights.

Design respects local architectural history. The main plaza has traditional building forms. The upper promenade and entry courts have a more restrained aesthetic in which simple walls form a backdrop for accents like a ceramic-tile fountain and wrought-iron detailing.

A muted color palette of sand, sage and putty blends with the desert's colors. Stucco, brick and brightly colored tile are used throughout, with wrought-iron and timber furnishings. Graphics for signs, directories, fountains and entry elements emphasize Southwestern art and craftsmanship.

La Encantada's public spaces host a variety of community events, including classes, concerts, parties and fund-raisers. Shopping and dining coexist easily with the public uses. One shopper noted that "The center reminds me of an elegant little village with the gardens and stairways. It seemed like a pretty place to hang out."

The developers say that La Encantada is an excellent example of "right growth," in which owners and the community engage in a development process of give-and-take and through which the community benefits from its new asset.

Traditional hot-climate design elements have been used, such as large roof overhangs, arcades, thick walls and interior courtyards.

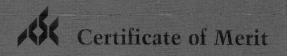 **Certificate of Merit**

Lafesta
Goyang, Gyeonggi, Korea

Owner:
Lafesta Proprietors' Union
Goyang, Gyeonggi, Korea

Management, Development and Leasing Company:
Chungwon Construction
Goyang, Gyeonggi, Korea

Design and Production Architect:
Haeahn Architecture, Inc.
Seoul, Korea

Graphic Designer:
CNM Interaktive
Seoul, Korea

Lighting Designer:
Nanam ALD
Seoul, Korea

Landscape Architect:
Group Teo
Seoul, Korea

General Contractor:
Byucksan Engineering & Construction Co., Ltd.
Seoul, Korea

Gross size of center:
747,174 sq. ft.

Gross leasable area (small shop space, excluding anchors):
391,636 sq. ft.

Total acreage of site:
5.3 acres

Type of center:
Regional lifestyle

Physical description:
Open-air

Center's trade area:
Urban Central Business District

Population:
- Primary trading area
  850,000

- Secondary trading area
  2,500,000

- Annualized percentage of shoppers anticipated to be from outside trade area
  5%

Development schedule:
- Opening date
  August 27, 2003

Parking spaces:
- 528

Lafesta lies in the central business district of Goyang, Korea.

*L*afesta is Korea's first lifestyle center, located in Goyang, an emerging suburb 12 miles northwest of Seoul.

The center was built on an underused site 1,082 feet (six blocks) long in Goyang's central business district. It offers both a variety of national-chain fashion and specialty retailers, as well as many venues for dining, leisure and entertainment.

After months of predesign research, the developers chose to

Lafesta assumes different personalities as the day wears on. From morning through midafternoon, adults from adjacent residential communities and office buildings visit Lafesta for lunch, shopping or exercise workouts. After school hours, teenagers wait in line for the live TV shows broadcast from the satellite kiosk of the Korea Music TV (KMTV) station, the nation's top-rated cable music station, which is on street level. Evenings bring families and people of all ages for entertainment and shopping.

KMTV anchors the entertainment section, which also includes an eight-screen multiplex cinema and an upscale fitness club. The center is laid out along the ground-floor promenade — a 50-foot-wide pedestrian boulevard where civic events are held daily. The Promenade has been referred to as Goyang's "living room." It is also a popular destination for residents of the region and tourists.

The design of the Promenade itself encourages repeat visits. Resilient recycled rubber — easy on shop-

build an open-air lateral configuration for the center's layout. This was unprecedented for Korea at the time, since major shopping centers had been stacked vertically. The design team instead planned a cluster of midrise buildings, positioned laterally — partially open-air along the central promenade. Detached buildings were connected on above-ground levels by a series of bridges in varying shapes — linear, circular or elliptical.

The bridges brought shoppers to upper-level arcades, visible from the ground, drawing shoppers to the upper levels of the multitiered facility. The sheltered bridges also serve as secondary balcony-like viewing sites for crowds attending the frequent concerts and festivals taking place in the street and plaza below.

Bridges (left) connecting various sections of the center also serve as secondary viewing sites for community events (right).

The center is accessible by car (above) and subways, drawing thousands for festivals and performances (right). Entertainment serves as a strong anchor for small shops (next page, far right) that are a welcome alternative to the big-box retailers available in other Korean shopping centers.

pers' feet — is used to tile the walkway floors. A large circle of natural-wood flooring in the middle of the Promenade becomes the stage for street music and dance performances, as well as a playground for skaters. Throughout the year, seasonal festivals are held, such as the Lake Flower Street Festival and the Arctic Sleigh Festival.

Streetscape elements such as a landscaped garden, fountains, sculpture, benches and kiosks complete the design of the center.

Lafesta's retail mix also varied from the established Korean norm. Previously, mall shoppers had to choose from big-box department stores and value retailers. At Lafesta, small shops, restaurants and the entertainment uses predominate.

Originally, location presented a problem. The Lafesta site was several blocks away from the major vehicular thoroughfares and subway stations and distant from other community gathering places. Designers conscientiously developed the entertainment and food functions to justify Lafesta as its own destination, unreliant on other attractions.

Recognizing Lafesta's unique needs, the developers kept the management and marketing teams on board after the center opened — contrary to the practice at other Korean shopping centers, where these functions transfer to individual storeowners upon the center's debut. The teams' continued attention to the community's needs has strengthened Lafesta's appeal.

MAJOR TENANTS		
NAME	**TYPE**	**GLA (SQ. FT.)**
Lotte Cinema	Eight-screen cinema	89,220
Rosen Brau	Restaurant	38,600
KMTV	Cable/music TV station	29,484
Bo Concept	Home furnishings	15,258
Bomnal Fitness	Fitness center	9,902
I.D Hair	Beauty salon	6,065

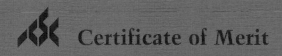
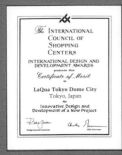

LaQua
Tokyo Dome City

Tokyo, Japan

Owner and Management Company:
Tokyo Dome KK
Tokyo, Japan

Design Architect:
RTKL Associates Inc.
Baltimore, Maryland, United States

Production Architect:
Takenaka Corporation
Tokyo, Japan

Graphic Designer:
RTKL Associates Inc.
Baltimore, Maryland, United States

Lighting Designer:
Matsushita Electrics
Osaka, Japan

General Contractor:
Takenaka Corporation
Tokyo, Japan

Development Company:
Takenaka Corporation
Tokyo, Japan

Leasing Company:
Tokyo Dome Corp.
Tokyo, Japan

Gross size of center:
584,000 sq. ft.

**Gross leasable area (small shop space,
excluding anchors):**
124,000 sq. ft.

Type of center:
Superregional theme

Physical description:
Multilevel open-air and enclosed mall

Center's trade area:
Urban Central Business District

Population:
- Primary trading area
  750,000

- Secondary trading area
  20,000,000

Development schedule:
- Opening date
  May 1, 2003

Parking spaces:
- 200

Photographs: Courtesy of Takenaka Corporation

*T*he owners of the Tokyo Dome stadium wanted to build an entertainment complex on an adjacent property to complement the Dome's 200 events each year. The result was LaQua Tokyo Dome City, offering entertainment, fine dining and event-day shopping.

Two oversized amusement features serve as icons for LaQua, both visible to passersby. There is a roller coaster, towering stories above the center and piercing the center's facade, adding a unique dimension to the downtown skyline. Equally dominant is the world's first center-less Ferris wheel.

An ancient hot spring covers 18,000 square feet beneath the site and complements the state-of-the-art spa comprising the center's top three levels (retail and restaurants are located on lower levels). The spa also inspired the central design theme. An aquatic motif informs the building's entire design. Information directories are shaped like water droplets. Whimsical aquatic inter-

The world's first center-less Ferris wheel and a roller coaster dominate the space above LaQua Tokyo Dome City.

The building exterior (top left) resembles a ship's bow. Inside, design incorporates an eclectic mix of plazas, trees, undulating water features and the ubiquitous amusement features.

MAJOR TENANTS

NAME	TYPE	GLA (SQ. FT.)
Seijo Ishii	Supermarket	9,956

pretations have been added to ceiling patterns and handrail accents. A waterlike form can be seen in the design of the building itself, as its sleek, rising form recalls images of a ship's graceful hull or a fin of a fish surfacing above water.

Designers faced several unusual challenges. The overarching issue was to create an architectural and graphic scheme that could effectively coordinate disparate elements like a spa and roller coaster. Also, the design would need to cater to all-day guests and short-term shoppers moving on to the Tokyo Dome stadium events. The site's dense urban setting would need to be addressed as well.

To respond to all these questions, the designers made sure that the center's now-bustling central plaza could be seen from every level. To accommodate the necessary but often unsightly safety structures of the thrill rides, the catchments of the Ferris wheel and roller coaster were made to look like a ship's sails. Safety barriers were crafted from stained wood to recall ship hulls.

Designers sought to create a unified narrative experience within the mall, rather than a traditional linear route. Water lent itself to the unified design, offering subtle changes in materials, textures, lighting and other design elements and allowing soft segues from areas of high activity to those with a more relaxed tempo. Bold wave shapes on the exterior convey the excitement of an amusement park, while gentler shapes and bubbling water features establish a quiet ambience in the spa.

The effective use of space to incorporate entertainment, retail and dining has been successful in developing a mixed clientele of businesspeople, families and tourists. Over 13 million people visited LaQua and its 70 shops, which include a Starbucks Coffee and a United Colors of Benetton, in its first nine months. Moreover, LaQua's success has actually reinvigorated the adjacent stadium, rather than just serving as a lengthener of event-focused trips.

Looking back, the key players believe that it would have been more efficient to bring in ancillary designers (landscapers, lighting designers and others) at the start of the process, rather than waiting until principal designers had created the concept. Because of that, some time was spent to overcome cultural and language differences to make sure all designers shared the same vision.

Nonetheless, the resulting LaQua represents a new way of looking at the functions of an urban retail center and a design concept that works with many uses.

Design amenities — lighting, water, glass, foliage — are seen everywhere at LaQua.

Signage (lower left) on water-droplet-like pylons reflects the overall water theme.

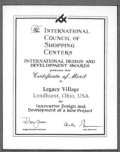

Legacy Village
Lyndhurst, Ohio, United States

Owner and Management Company:
First-Interstate Properties, Ltd.
Lyndhurst, Ohio, United States

Design and Production Architect:
Dorsky Hodgson Parrish Yue
Cleveland, Ohio, United States

Graphic Designer:
Dorsky Hodgson Parrish Yue
Cleveland, Ohio, United States

Lighting Designer:
The Lighting Practice
Philadelphia, Pennsylvania, United States

Landscape Architect:
Mahan Rykiel Associates, Inc.
Baltimore, Maryland, United States

General Contractor:
Independence Excavating, Inc.
Independence, Ohio, United States

Development Company:
First-Interstate Properties, Ltd.
Lyndhurst, Ohio, United States

Leasing Company:
Goodman Real Estate Services Group, LLC
Lyndhurst, Ohio, United States

Gross size of center:
615,000 sq. ft.

Gross leasable area (small shop space, excluding anchors):
615,000 sq. ft.

Total acreage of site:
70 acres

Type of center:
Lifestyle

Physical description:
Three-level open-air

Center's trade area:
Suburban

Population:
- Primary trading area
  447,756

- Secondary trading area
  1,215,337

- Annualized percentage of shoppers anticipated to be from outside trade area
  25%

Development schedule:
- Opening date
  October 2003

Parking spaces:
- 2,576

*L*egacy Village is a three-story mixed-use lifestyle center in northeast Ohio — the area's first. The center, encompassing shopping, dining, entertainment and office space, is built in a Main Street configuration with landscaped plazas, miniparks and rich streetscape amenities.

Having studied examples of recently built traditional town centers, the designers chose to create their Main Street concept by carefully arranging buildings and streets around a series of pub-

lic spaces, blending architectural styles, materials and details to achieve the diversity of early small towns that evolved over time.

The site had previously held an estate, and the main entry is reminiscent of that use — an old estate entrance with gated entry points, an axial entry drive flanked by parts of the original stone walls and a ceremonial fountain, with the main buildings at the end of the vistas.

The historic ambience continues into the center itself through the choices of light fixtures, benches and decorative bollards. Environmental graphics, banners and street signs reinforce the old estate style. The color palette is kept to earth tones with many gabled roofs among a wide variety.

Legacy Village responds to physical limitations imposed by the site: The center is essentially sculpted into the land. The regimented grid layout typically associated with Main Street formats

Photograph: Taxel Image Group

An aerial view (right) shows the main road leading to the shops of Legacy Village in northeast Ohio. Streetlights and side-walks (above) introduce the sense of community to shoppers.

Photograph: First Interstate Properties, Ltd.

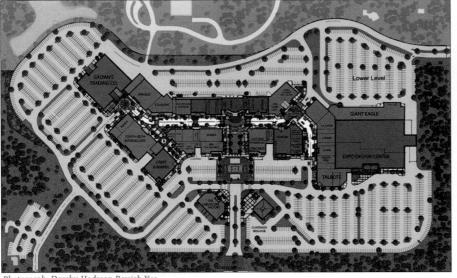

Photograph: Dorsky Hodgson Parrish Yue

Photograph: Abel Photographics

Photograph: Taxel Image Group

Photograph: Taxel Image Group

Photograph: Dorsky Hodgson Parrish Yue

MAJOR TENANTS

NAME	TYPE	GLA (SQ. FT.)
EXPO Design Center	Home	90,900
Dick's Sporting Goods	Sporting goods	81,665
Giant Eagle	Supermarket	80,363
Crate&Barrel	Home	35,925
Joseph-Beth Booksellers	Bookstore	26,628

Site constrictions did not inhibit the imagination of designers in creating a center that looks like Main Street.

here contains angles and curves along the streets. This approach allows visitors to discover the space through various vistas.

The designers encouraged tenants to express their own identity and design styles through their infill design, signage and detail. Use of design zones specified hierarchical areas of major and secondary architectural impact.

To accommodate the harsh Ohio winters, 70,000 square feet of heating cables are built into the sidewalk to melt ice and snow, allowing comfortable and safe pedestrian movement along the storefronts. Wind tunnel analyses located hot spots where excessive wind speed could occur, and the layouts of buildings were modified to reduce drafts and enhance shopper comfort even in severe weather.

The large supermarket could have broken the Main Street design concept with a store exterior that resembled a group of buildings rather than a traditional boxlike structure. Positioning the grocery store directly below a conventional retail anchor gave maximum use of the site. The dramatic change in grade called for creative solutions to resolve some complex requirements in the mechanical system.

The site constrictions also led to building an underground parking garage connecting to second-level retailers and third-level offices via elevators.

The developers sought to make Legacy Village a community asset. They engaged all stakeholders from the start, including civic leadership, retailers and eventually over 100 contractors. Not losing sight of its role as a corporate citizen, the owner has built charitable opportunities into the center's operation. The grand opening served as a benefit for the American Red Cross and two local charities. The center's Change for Charity program donates funds to local nonprofit groups from the use of parking meters.

Legacy Village mixes a range of well-known retailers with a supermarket and more than a dozen food/restaurant choices to produce a center focused on community in both design and function.

Photograph: Taxel Image Group

Streetlights (right) enhance the design by day and night.

Photograph: Taxel Image Group

Gabled roofs (below) are plentiful above the three-story mixed-use buildings.

Photograph: Abel Photographics

Photograph: Taxel Image Group

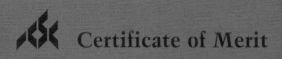

Namba Parks
Osaka, Japan

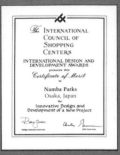

Owner and Management Company:
Nankai Electric Railway Co., LTD.
Osaka, Japan

Design Architect:
The Jerde Partnership
Venice, California, United States

Production Architect:
Obayashi Corporation
Osaka, Japan

Graphic Designer:
Bikousha
Osaka, Japan

Lighting Designer:
Matsushita Electrics
Osaka, Japan

Landscape Architect:
Tsujimoto Ryushouen
Osaka, Japan

General Contractor:
Obayashi Corporation
Osaka, Japan

Development and Leasing Companies:
Nankai Electric Railway Co., LTD.
Osaka, Japan
Takashimaya
Osaka, Japan

Gross size of center:
430,571 sq. ft.

Gross leasable area (small shop space, excluding anchors):
263,724 sq. ft.

Total acreage of site:
8.33 acres

Type of center:
Fashion/Lifestyle/Entertainment

Physical description:
Eight-level open-air and enclosed mall

Center's trade area:
Urban Central Business District

Population:
- Primary trading area
  3,000,000

- Secondary trading area
  12,000,000

- Annualized percentage of shoppers anticipated to be from outside trade area
  10%-15%

Development schedule:
- Opening date
  October 2003

Parking spaces:
- 363

*O*saka, Japan — one of the most densely populated cities in the world — gets a much-needed natural amenity in Namba Parks, a new mixed-use urban lifestyle center located on an underused eight-acre parcel in the city's central business district. The center is anchored visually by a 30-story office tower.

The site is surrounded by raised railroad tracks to the east and an urban boulevard and elevated viaduct to the west. It was once occupied by Osaka Stadium: the center's paving now contains replicas of a home plate and pitcher's rubber to commemorate the site's history.

A rooftop park — the site's most unique feature — does not merely sit atop the building, but rather uses a sloped design that ascends eight levels to allow the park to be seen from the streets below, drawing visitors into the mall. The 2.8 acre park is one of Osaka's largest, and contains trees, miniature ponds, shrubbery and planting beds, all irrigated by recycled water filtered from the mall's restaurants.

The design concept is of a canyon coursing through the urban park, with 108 shops and restaurants in close proximity to the greenery. The "canyon" is built from bands of colored stone and reinforces the project's connection with nature while forming the primary circulation path through the retail areas. The path is sculpted to create a sense of mystery, with coves, caves, valleys and other places to be explored. Glass bridges connect

Meant to suggest a canyon winding through shopping areas, Namba Parks in downtown Osaka, Japan, provides an urban park in the crowded city.

MAJOR TENANTS

NAME	TYPE	GLA (SQ. FT.)
Sports Authority	Sporting goods	53,821

The canyon effect comes from bands of colored stone and offers many coves, caves and other areas to be explored as it wends its way through the center's eight levels. Glass-enclosed bridges span the canyon.

the two sides of the canyon and at night become arched tubes of light. All vertical spaces are sky-lit from the open-air park above.

Shoppers access the project's main interior spaces through a "figure-8" circulation path that crosses the canyon through the glass

bridges, leading to the sloped park plane. The path repeatedly allows visitors to continue shopping or instead take a break in the park. A series of plazas each contain a water feature or other attraction.

The rooftop park also serves as an important environmental function. Osaka has become a "heat island" — the city's summer temperatures are hotter than those in surrounding communities. According to the contractor's tests, the midday surface temperatures of the park's green areas averaged 62 degrees cooler than the asphalt surfaces of rooftop parking lots and highways nearby. The amount of heat transmitted into the city by the rooftop park was one-tenth of the heat of the nongreen areas.

At the center of the project is a terraced amphitheater, a three-story organic space, embellished with greenery, foliage and water, that serves as a public entertainment venue. The underside of the

nearby hemispheric crown of the elevator tower offers a laser light show during the evening.

The retail spaces in Namba Parks are filled by popular midscale and upscale Japanese and international chains. Shops are typically under 3,000 square feet. The anchor is a three-story Sports Authority. The mall has no central food court. Rather, restaurants are located to take advantage of rooftop terraces and city views.

The project's second phase will add entertainment venues to Namba Parks in an attempt to lengthen visits by residents and tourists staying at a nearby hotel, who were tending to leave to look for cinemas, amusement parlors and the like. As it grows, Namba Parks will continue to serve the public's retail and recreation needs through innovative design.

The rooftop parks (top right) serve environmental purposes as well. Plazas (center) are used for community presentations. The greenery in the Namba Parks canyon (bottom right) offers welcome respite in one of Japan's most densely populated regions.

Some areas (left) blend nature and commerce. Others (below) are purely shopping venues.

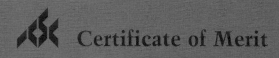

The Shops at Legacy

Plano, Texas, United States

Owner:
The Shops at Legacy L.P.
Plano, Texas, United States

Management Company:
The Karahan Companies
Plano, Texas, United States

Design and Production Architect:
RTKL Associates Inc.
Dallas, Texas, United States

Graphic Designer:
RTKL Associates Inc.
Baltimore, Maryland, United States

Lighting Designer:
T. Kondos Associates
New York, New York, United States

Landscape Architect:
Huitt Zollars, Inc./Land Patterns
Dallas, Texas, United States

General Contractors:
Manhattan Construction
Rogers-O'Brien Construction
Dallas, Texas, United States

Development Company:
The Karahan Companies
Dallas, Texas, United States

Leasing Company:
The Karahan Companies/Open Realty Advisors
Plano, Texas, United States

Gross size of center:
315,000 sq. ft.

Gross leasable area (small shop space, excluding anchors):
268,000 sq. ft.

Total acreage of site:
165 acres

Type of center:
Mixed-use lifestyle

Physical description:
Open-air

Center's trade area:
Suburban

Population:
- Primary trading area
  250,800
- Secondary trading area
  513,000

Development schedule:
- Opening date
  June 23, 2004

Parking spaces:
- 1,366

Photographs: Courtesy of Charles Davis Smith, AIA

The Shops at Legacy provides the commercial spine of Plano, Texas, offering streetscale development rare to the suburban sprawl that characterizes this area north of Dallas.

The site had previously been a large and empty plot of land between the Dallas North Tollway and a large corporate office park. Lacking any reason to stay, the 36,000 office employees would drive away at day's end.

Developed during a time when two major single-use regional mall projects were being built within a two-mile radius, The Shops at Legacy offers a sustainable, mixed-use alternative.

The center integrates an eclectic mix of retail, restaurants and entertainment uses with upper-level office space, creating a Main Street feel. On-site parking enhances a pedestrian-oriented layout and serves as a traffic buffer. Sidewalks end at a tree-lined lakefront park adjacent to a

The Shops at Legacy are part of a mixed-use project, bringing street-scale design to the sprawling Texas plains.

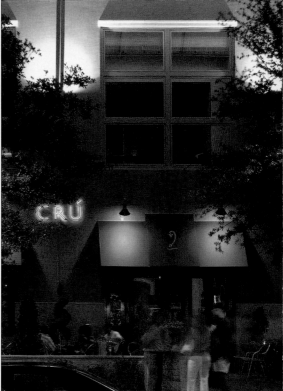

Street parking (above) allows easy access to stores. Additional parking off-street is visually shielded but clearly marked.

MAJOR TENANTS

NAME	TYPE	GLA (SQ. FT.)
Robb & Stucky	Furniture	115,000
Angelika Film Center & Cafe	——	30,000
AchieveGlobal	Consulting firm	9,482
Bob's Steak Chop House	Restaurant	7,793
Benchmark Bank	Bank	7,062

Marriott Hotel and corporate campus facilities.

Legacy Drive splits the center's site as a major east-west connector road lined with on-site parking and retail. Parking lots and decks are screened from direct views from the main spine, but clearly identified and accessible, allowing for both pleasing aesthetics and ease of traffic and pedestrian flow.

As to the streetscape itself, the designers resisted the old-time America look popular among many new open centers in favor of a contemporary vision of various historical styles and forms within the scale of traditional downtowns. Mixed and matched towers, canopies and facade treatments along the street combine to achieved the desired variety.

Landscapers and other designers paid close attention to the oft-searing summer heat of the Texas plains. Tree limbs start above the height of passersby, providing shade. Storefront canopies and the presence of second-story offices also protect against sunlight as shoppers peer into store windows.

Awnings, rooftop facades and door and window treatments are as diverse as one would find in a downtown that had evolved naturally. Signage, in particular, shows variety. A store sign flattened

against the building might be next door to another that evokes sculpture, which in turn might be next to one hanging off the building's side, calling out to pedestrians a half-block away.

The Shops at Legacy is the retail component of the mixed-use Legacy Town Center project. The retail component actually followed the initial residential development due to the fact that the residential market was more attractive than the retail at the time the master plan of the project was implemented. As a result, retail priorities did not drive the creation of the master plan, which the retail developer would have preferred. Nonetheless, the retail integrates seamlessly with the entertainment, office and residential uses of the project to create a live-work environment to the benefit of all.

Signage, window treatments and awnings (right) lend the look of a downtown that might have evolved naturally.

Extensive landscaping and awnings make The Shops at Legacy a pleasant environment.

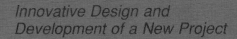
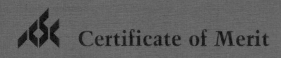

Certificate of Merit

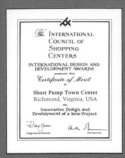

Short Pump Town Center

Richmond, Virginia, United States

Owners:
Forest City Enterprises
Cleveland, Ohio, United States
MJGT Associates
Richmond, Virginia, United States

Management Company:
Forest City Commercial Management
Cleveland, Ohio, United States

Design Architect:
Thompson, Ventulett, Stainback & Associates
Atlanta, Georgia, United States

Production Architect:
KA, Inc.
Cleveland, Ohio, United States

Graphic Designer:
Huie Design, Inc.
Atlanta, Georgia, United States

Lighting Designer:
Bliss Fasman, Inc.
New York, New York, United States

Landscape Architects:
Roy Ashley & Associates
Atlanta, Georgia, United States
SWA Group
Sausalito, California, United States

General Contractor:
Whiting-Turner Contracting Company
Baltimore, Maryland, United States

Development Companies:
Forest City Commercial Development
Cleveland, Ohio, United States
MJGT Associates
Richmond, Virginia, United States

Leasing Company:
Forest City Retail Leasing
Cleveland, Ohio, United States

Photographs: Brian Gassel/TVS.
(All photos except top right on page 79 and page 81.)

Gross size of center:
1,181,000 sq. ft.

Gross leasable area (small shop space, excluding anchors):
411,000 sq. ft.

Total acreage of site:
147 acres

Type of center:
Regional lifestyle

Physical description:
Two-level open-air

Center's trade area:
Suburban

Population:
- Primary trading area
  195,000
- Secondary trading area
  489,000
- Annualized percentage of shoppers
  anticipated to be from outside trade area
  5%

Development schedule:
- Opening date
  September 4, 2003

Parking spaces:
- 5,250

The two-level Short Pump Town Center outside historic Richmond, Virginia, blends storefront diversity, extensive landscaping and pedestrian comfort to hint at America's Main Street.

Short Pump Town Center is a new two-level open-air lifestyle center 12 miles from historic Richmond, Virginia. The project features pedestrian streets, spacious courts and plazas. Building facades are carefully articulated and scaled. Each building has its own detailing and image but has been kept in comfortable relation to adjacent buildings to give the impression that the block had evolved over an extended period of time.

The center puts high priority on shopper comfort. Arcades and canopies throughout the entire open-air center allow shopping visits to continue despite inclement weather. Grassy lawns are used for picnics. Overall, Short Pump blends the retail mix of a traditional upscale mall with the look of an open-air mercantile street. It is a comfortable pedestrian-oriented community within a community that invites visitors to linger. Vehicles are kept to the center's exterior, allowing the avenues and plazas to be used exclusively by pedestrians.

An interactive fountain features a raised basin with seating around the edges. Water flows into the pool from a short-handled pump supplied by stone troughs radiating from the center of the fountain. The pool is surrounded by smaller flowing pumps in different sizes and colors.

To foster local residents' sense of identification with the project, the designers sought architectural integrity and richness of detail, which could have easily become costly. Instead, they used a "kit of parts" concept, in which the project was divided into six major building groups. The two-story facades in each group were subdivided into 75 expressions created from a select palette of component pieces. The kit offered facade variations through the use of shape, material, color and finish. Continuity was reinforced through scale, details, textures and the recurrence of streetlights, furniture, handrails, paving materials, graphics/signage and extensive landscaping.

History and visual appeal abound at Short Pump Town Center. An obelisk is topped by a statue of singer Ella Fitzgerald in a tribute to the first lady of jazz. Another statue honors Native Americans.

Designers offered retailers a "kit-of-parts" design concept to achieve variety within a consistent look. The "short pump" of the center's name can be seen at upper right.

Streetlamps reaching nearly to the second floor are reminiscent of old gaslamps. Metallic blackbirds seem ready to fly from a sign pylon. The center's name itself comes from a local tavern under whose porch stood a short-handled pump — locals would say, "See you at the Short Pump."

Landscaping was enhanced soon after the Short Pump opened. The initial installation minimized landscaping in favor of better sight lines to tenant storefronts. Shoppers, however, wanted a softer look to their surroundings, so more greenery was added — with tenants' blessings.

Upper levels in open-air retail centers often suffer from lack of traffic, but Short Pump addressed that challenge with extensive and convenient access to the top level. Two of the seven entrances from surrounding parking lead directly to the upper level. Three department stores also have entries from the top floor. Six sets of covered escalators, three passenger elevators at different locations and stairs offer ample vertical access. Also, the centrally located second-level food court serves to bring shoppers up.

County government supported Short Pump's success by creating a Community Development Authority to pay for $22 million in improvements to roadways and utilities for the project. The center won the award as Most Significant Virginia Real Estate Project of 2003 from the Virginia chapter of Certified Commercial Investment Members, who cited Short Pump as "a high-impact project in terms of economic impact on the market."

Short Pump Town Center has more than 120 retail units, 40 percent of which are new to Richmond. An anchor department store withdrew from the project,

Architectural detail and extensive landscaping (top and right), plus food and family togetherness (below) create a community experience at Short Pump Town Center.

Photograph: Henry Spiker/TVS.

MAJOR TENANTS		
NAME	**TYPE**	**GLA (SQ. FT.)**
Dillard's	Department store	230,000
Hecht's	Department store	200,000
Nordstrom	Department store	120,000
Dick's Sporting Goods	Sporting goods	81,000

prompting the developer to plan Short Pump Phase II, with an additional 77,000 square feet. In all, the developers achieved their goal of providing the underserved Richmond market with a high-quality retail experience.

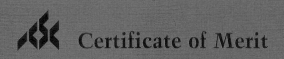

Terramall Shopping Center

San Jose, Costa Rica

Owner and Management Company:
Grupo Bursatil Aldesa
San Jose, Costa Rica

Design Architect:
Beame Architectural Partnership
Coral Gables, Florida, United States

Production Architect:
Ossenbach, Pendones & Bonilla
San Jose, Costa Rica

Graphic Designer:
Redmond Schwartz Mark Design
San Clemente, California, United States

Lighting Designer:
T. Kondos Associates
New York, New York, United States

General Contractor:
Constructora van der Laat y Jimenez
San Jose, Costa Rica

Development and Leasing Company:
Grupo Bursatil Aldesa
San Jose, Costa Rica

Gross size of center:
501,213 sq. ft.

Gross leasable area (small shop space, excluding anchors):
369,788 sq. ft.

Total acreage of site:
18 acres

Type of center:
Regional

Physical description:
Three-level enclosed mall

Center's trade area:
Urban but not Central Business District

Population:
- Primary trading area
  753,093

- Secondary trading area
  867,767

- Annualized percentage of shoppers anticipated to be from outside trade area
  10%

Development schedule:
- Opening date
  October 30, 2003

Parking spaces:
- 1,200

*T*erramall in San Jose, Costa Rica, is indeed "of the land," as its name implies. The three-level regional shopping center is nestled into the hillside of an existing coffee plantation with views of Carpintera Mountain, one of the nation's most beautiful natural preservation sites.

The designers' mission was, in fact, to blend the shopping center into the landscape, providing an icon from a passing expressway, a pedestrian-scaled entry from local streets and a series of natural spatial interior environments that called for shoppers' exploration.

At the knoll of the property, what was once a dramatic and unexpected view of the Carpintera experienced only by foot became a stepped outdoor plaza named La Vereda — an amphitheater offering exceptional views. The cinemas are located at the end of this plaza to allow the Terramall's entertainment section to operate independently at night. The building profile slopes with the surrounding mountains and hills, reflecting the geometries of the natural spaces.

Photograph: BAP

Photograph: Thomas Delbeck

Terramall Shopping Center in San Jose, Costa Rica, is nestled into a mountainside and is oriented to take advantage of the area's breezes and lighting.

Photograph: Thomas Delbeck

Outside or in, Terramall brings new dimensions of retailing to eastern San Jose.

Photograph: Thomas Delbeck

Photograph: Thomas Delbeck

Photograph: BAP

Photograph: Thomas Delbeck

MAJOR TENANTS

NAME	TYPE	GLA (SQ. FT.)
Cinepolis	Multiscreen cinema	76,000
Arliss	Department store	41,000
Permercados	Supermarket	19,700
Tommy Hilfiger	Clothing	8,200
Ming	——	3,200

To achieve the greatest retail strength, developers included a major retail "event" on each level. On the first floor, a supermarket and market plaza serve as the main entry; the market is wrapped by service retailers. The second level is anchored at one end by a food court and at the other by two major tenants.

The third floor — the largest — includes the strongest anchors and the entertainment plaza. This level is stepped back from the second retail level below, so tenant signs would be visible from all locations on either level. Storefronts on the third level were required to be taller to maximize tenant identity from floors below.

Construction presented several challenges. The site slopes 60 feet down the long side of a hill — flat floors were problematic. The answer was that the three-level mall plan would have entries from direct and convenient parking.

Costa Rica's hot and rainy climate also proved troublesome. There is daily rain during much of the year. Electric power is costly, discouraging use of air-conditioning. The answer came in the positioning of the building. Its site orientation takes advantage of natural breezes and uses natural light. The roof is shaped to encourage air movement while sheltering shoppers from the

daily rainfall. Openings below the roof and entries catch the breezes. Skylights and clerestory windows bring natural accent lighting.

The site is also in a seismic zone — an active volcano is nearby. Therefore, a rigid concrete structural system was used inside tenant spaces, and a light, airy roof system was used in place of a typical ceiling.

The mix of entertainment, good design and retailing is particularly strong at Terramall. The surrounding area lacked restaurants and entertainment amenities, prompting developers to focus on these aspects, including some of the best-known national food venues and bistros. The 15-screen cinema has stadium seating and a luxurious VIP section that serves meals and offers wide leather seats.

Terramall has become the heart of its community, say the developers, stressing shopper appeal and lifestyle amenities even as it breaks with Costa Rica's traditional retailing styles.

Covered walkways (top right) provide protection from Costa Rica's hot sun and daily rain.

Designers made sure there was a retail attraction on each of the mall's three levels to encourage longer visits. Crowds (below) testify to the developer's success in making Terramall the heart of its community.

All photographs on this page: Thomas Delbeck

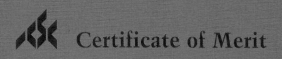

Triangle
Town Center

Raleigh, North Carolina, United States

Owner and Management Company:
Richard E. Jacobs Group, Inc.
Cleveland, Ohio, United States

Design and Production Architect:
Thompson, Ventulett, Stainback & Associates
Atlanta, Georgia, United States

Graphic Designer:
Callison
Seattle, Washington, United States

Lighting Designer:
T. Kondos Associates
New York, New York, United States

Landscape Architect:
MESA Design
Dallas, Texas, United States

General Contractor:
Hoar Construction
Birmingham, Alabama, United States

Development and Leasing Company:
Richard E. Jacobs Group, Inc.
Cleveland, Ohio, United States

Gross size of center:
1,587,356 sq. ft.

Gross leasable area (small shop space, excluding anchors):
1,439,242 sq. ft.

Total acreage of site:
131.1 acres

Type of center:
Regional

Physical description:
Enclosed mall

Center's trade area:
Suburban

Population:
• Primary trading area
 468,353

• Secondary trading area
 649,691

• Annualized percentage of shoppers
 anticipated to be from outside trade area
 15%

Development schedule:
• Opening date
 August 14, 2002

Parking spaces:
• 6,537

*Creekside Cafes — a
food court and per-
formance area — is
one of five sections
of Triangle Town
Center in Raleigh,
North Carolina.*

*T*riangle Town Center in Raleigh, North Carolina, is a hybrid center, offering five department store anchors, an outdoor commons with shops and restaurants and an adjacent power center.

There are five zones — or "experiences" — at Triangle Town Center: Triangle Town Commons, Market Street, the Traditional Mall, the Contemporary Mall and the Creekside Cafes.

Triangle Town Commons is an outdoor collection of shops and restaurants that lead to the mall's main entrance. Its identity comes from its festive atmosphere, its central plaza and a manmade river flowing through its center. This section's design uses the site's natural stone and hundreds of varieties of shrubs, trees and grasses. Triangle Town Commons is the setting for concerts, arts festivals and community events.

Market Street, just inside the main entrance, is a collection of

Hungry shoppers at the Creekside Cafes (above) can choose between inside and outside dining areas.

Triangle Town Commons (below and below right) is a collection of shops and restaurants that line the entry-way to the mall.

Designed to be quiet and elegant, it is the home for upscale shops and department stores. Columns are covered with colored stone; railings are made with cherry wood, stainless steel and glass; and Italian marble tile is used on the lower level.

The Contemporary Mall makes up the center's west wing. Above, shoppers see a tilted, serpentine ceiling dotted with unusual skylights. Railings are sleek, angular stainless steel and glass. Floors are covered with carpet in abstract patterns or in marble. This section includes stores for children and family merchandise. A soft-sculpture play area — Curiosity Creek — is designed to remind shoppers of the old swimming hole of American lore.

Finally, the Creekside Cafes is the food court, where shoppers can dine indoors or on the mall's outdoor park plaza. Naturalized pools remind diners of a riverside picnic area. Shoppers often remove their shoes and wade in an outdoor fountain. This section includes a performance stage.

Among the many nature-inspired aspects of the Triangle Town Center design, water is the major component. Beyond the manmade river and natural rock bed in the Triangle Town Commons, there is

a waterfall in the central court and the wading pool at the food court. Nature paths and bike trails wend their way through the 9,000 trees on the property. In all, nearly half the project site is green space.

The surroundings were even included in the construction materials. The developer created a rock-crushing plant during the earliest phases, so much of the rock could be used at the base of the mall's parking areas. Many of the boulders were used as landscaping accents. A boulder — the "Triangle Stone" — was preserved during construction. Made of 7.5 tons of solid granite, the boulder was placed in the Creekside Cafes area to represent the millions of years of the earth's history and the enduring character of the region.

Befitting its role as a new destination for the community, Triangle Town Center has conducted several fund-raising and awareness events for groups such as Habitat for Humanity, the Society for the Prevention of Cruelty to Animals (SPCA) and the American Cancer Society. Between its retail mix and varied design, Triangle Town Center has proven to be a valuable addition to this rapidly growing region.

glass-enclosed specialty shops. It is the only one-level area of the mall and reminds shoppers of a friendly downtown street of eclectic shops and restaurants. Overhead festival lights add to the atmosphere. A Barnes & Noble Superstore anchors this section.

The Traditional Mall comprises the east wing of the center.

Views of the Contemporary Mall section (above) show the serpentine ceiling and the old swimming-hole motif of the soft-sculpture play area. Below (from left), the Creekside Cafes food court, the festival lights in the Market Street section and the Contemporary Mall area show the varied design experience at Triangle Town Center.

MAJOR TENANTS		
NAME	**TYPE**	**GLA (SQ. FT.)**
Dillard's	Department store	206,000
Belk	Department store	180,230
Hecht's	Department store	179,930
Sears	Department store	144,846
Saks Fifth Avenue	Department store	83,066
Dick's Sporting Goods	Sporting goods	75,000

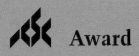

SouthPark Mall

Charlotte, North Carolina, United States

Owner and Management Company:
Simon Property Group
Indianapolis, Indiana, United States

Design Architects:
Bartlett Associates MegaStrategies
LS3P ASSOCIATES LTD.
Charlotte, North Carolina, United States

Production Architect:
LS3P ASSOCIATES LTD.
Charlotte, North Carolina, United States

Graphic Designers:
LS3P ASSOCIATES LTD.
Bartlett Associates MegaStrategies
Charlotte, North Carolina, United States

Lighting Designers:
MCLA-Inc.
Washington, DC, United States
Randy Burkett Lighting Design
St. Louis, Missouri, United States

Landscape Architects:
LandDesign
Charlotte, North Carolina, United States
Site Works
Birmingham, Alabama, United States

General Contractor:
FN Thompson/Pinnix
Charlotte, North Carolina, United States

Development and Leasing Company:
Simon Property Group
Indianapolis, Indiana, United States

Gross size of center:
- Before renovation/expansion
  1,193,151 sq. ft.
- After renovation/expansion
  1,498,261 sq. ft.

Current gross leasable area (small shop space, including anchors):
1,416,225 sq. ft.

Total acreage of site:
95.5 acres

Type of center:
Superregional center

Physical description:
One-level open-air and enclosed mall

Center's trade area:
Suburban

Population:
- Primary trading area
  695,000
- Secondary trading area
  600,000
- Annualized percentage of shoppers anticipated to be from outside trade area
  16.6%

Development schedule:
- Opening date
  1970
- Current renovation/expansion date
  March 2004

Parking spaces:
- Present number
  6,550
- Number added in renovation/expansion
  1,177

A fountain and outdoor glass gallery topped by an 85-foot-high glass dome now welcomes shoppers to SouthPark Mall in Charlotte, North Carolina.

Photograph: Tim Buchman

Photography: Sanborn (Aerial Surveys - Digital Mapping)

MAJOR TENANTS		
NAME	TYPE	GLA (SQ. FT.)
Belk	Department store	336,598
Dillards	Department store	225,881
Hecht's	Department store	200,000
Nordstrom	Department store	145,185
Dick's Sporting Goods	Sporting goods	84,000

An aerial view of SouthPark Mall (left) shows new deck parking. Entry roads old (left center) and new (below) lead to the porte cochere at the main entrance (lower left).

Photograph: Mitchell Kearney

Photograph: Tim Buchman

Photograph: Tim Buchman

SouthPark, a mall in the growing metropolis of Charlotte, North Carolina, was built in 1960. Renovated and expanded in the early 1980's, it had gotten a tired, outdated look. The economic and population growth of the Charlotte area offered substantial opportunities for SouthPark Mall, and its owner decided to renovate and expand again to transform the mall into an elegant shopping destination.

Expansion took place in seven phases. The first was to create Symphony Park, which has become home to the Charlotte Summer Pops Concerts. The owner built a permanent 136-foot clear-span tensile structure and stage over a lake in a seven-acre park, which accommodates up to 18,000 people for concerts.

Phase two was the new entryway at East Plaza Gallery, a central outdoor glass structure and porte cochere topped by an 85-foot-tall glass dome. The Cheesecake Factory and Maggiano's Little Italy restaurants flank the gallery, which is 423 feet long and offers lush landscaping, pedestrianscale lighting, brick sidewalks and a traditional fountain.

Renovation of the existing SouthPark Mall constituted phase three. The entire gray-tiled floor was replaced with German limestone. Columns and bulkheads of courts are now clad by dark cherry panels with maple trim. Many soft seating areas were added and built-in planters removed. A new central foundation with granite

Before-and-after pictures of the mall exterior (top), interior (center) and food court (below) show how column cladding, landscaping, awnings and rooftop moldings add design value.

All photographs on this page: Tim Buchman

Photograph: Tim Buchman

Design plans for the new luxury wing (above) attracted upscale tenants. Natural lighting (below) floods a mall area and anchor court.

Photograph: Tim Buchman

cladding entertains shoppers with its continuous preset water show.

Phase four was to expand the mall with new Nordstrom and Neiman Marcus anchor stores and 90,000 square feet of small shop space.

Photograph: Tim Buchman

Photograph: Mitchell Kearney

Photograph: Mitchell Kearney

Photograph: LS3P

The finishes in phase three were carried into phase four's luxury shopping environment. Ceilings in this section are higher and articulated with maple panels, allowing storefronts to extend to the new heights sought by tenants. These plans attracted upscale tenants such as Tiffany & Co., Louis Vuitton and Burberry.

The former food court location was a retrofit at the intersection of two coordinators, lacking any identity. In phase five, the food court was moved to an outside portion of the mall looking toward Symphony Park. Designers removed existing structure to create a grand clerestory, allowing light to flood the white-tiled space. Columns were clad with white subway-style tile and pewter capitals, recalling the atmosphere of Victorian-era conservatories. Vendors were asked to make their counter areas as open as possible to reinforce the light, airy feeling. Chandeliers, sconces and ceiling fans accent the overhead space.

Phase six — the new west plaza entrance — required the purchase and demolition of a former Sears department store. The new entrance is a lifestyle plaza surrounded by restaurants, outdoor dining, a bookstore and a high-end

Photograph: LS3P

Photograph: LS3P

sporting goods store. The plaza has transformed what had been called "the back of the mall" into an extensive landscaped plaza centered on a grand fountain.

The final phase added three parking decks to the mall. Designers tied the decks to the architectural design concepts used in the mall's interior, including facades, canopies and special lighting in the east entrance gallery.

Photograph: LS3P

Photograph: LS3P

Outdated and low-visibility signage (upper left) gave way to clearer directional graphics, particularly for the new parking decks.

Photograph: Tim Buchman

Two years of oft-contentious rezoning deliberations preceded SouthPark Mall's renovation and expansion. The mall's owner/ developer and designers worked closely with city planners to create an environment that is pedestrian-friendly and economically supportive of the area.

All work that would affect shoppers was done when the mall was closed at night. Areas under construction were barricaded or cleaned every morning before shoppers' arrival. Community interest in the renovation caused mall sales to increase during construction.

The grand-opening galas were tied to community charities and sold out overnight. Local media publicized the events. Advertising campaigns in *Time* magazine and *Architectural Digest* magazine announced the renovation and expansion, spotlighting new tenants. The ads used a construction motif to raise patrons' curiosity and help them buy into the changes.

Photograph: Tim Buchman

The first Christmas tree lighting event after reopening attracted 11,000 people, and affluent shoppers who used to make weekend retail flights to New York City now stay home, showing that through renovation, expansion and a new tenant mix, SouthPark Mall has become a destination for shopping, entertainment and community events.

Photograph: Rick Alexander

The new west plaza entrance (far left, top) transformed what used to be "the back of the mall." Inside, plentiful landscaping, soft seating areas and water features (left and below) create a shopper-friendly ambience.

The huge canopy at Symphony Park (above) and a glass dome (below) add new accents to the skyline around SouthPark Mall.

Photograph: Mitchell Kearney

Photograph: Tim Buchman

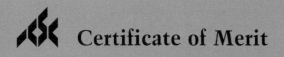
Americana Manhasset

Manhasset, New York, United States

Owner and Management Company:
Castagna Realty Co.
Manhasset, New York, United States

Design and Production Architect:
Peter Marino Architects
New York, New York, United States

Graphic Designer:
Castagna Realty Co.
Manhasset, New York, United States

Lighting Designer:
Johnson Schwinghammer Lighting Consultants, Inc.
New York, New York, United States

Landscape Architect:
Oehme, van Sweden & Associates, Inc.
Washington, DC, United States

General Contractor:
RFC Construction Corp., an affiliate of Castagna Realty Co.
Manhasset, New York, United States

Development Company:
Fifth Avenue of L. I. Realty Co./Castagna Realty Co.
Manhasset, New York, United States

Leasing Company:
Siegel Consultants Ltd.
Huntington, New York, United States

Gross size of center:
- Before renovation/expansion
214,308 sq. ft.
- After renovation/expansion
217,824 sq. ft.

Current gross leasable area (small shop space, excluding anchors):
217,824 sq. ft.

Total acreage of site:
12.6 acres

Type of center:
Lifestyle

Physical description:
One-level open-air

Center's trade area:
Suburban

Population:
- Primary trading area
2,240,230
- Secondary trading area
3,302,225
- Annualized percentage of shoppers anticipated to be from outside trade area
9.9%

Development schedule:
- Opening date
1956
- Current renovation/expansion date
August 2003

Parking spaces:
- Present number
1,255
- None added in renovation/expansion

*O*pened in 1956, Americana Manhasset is an open-air shopping center on Long Island, New York. Originally, the center included two supermarkets and a five-and-dime store. Other, more upscale, tenants had been attracted to the center over the years by the increasing affluence of the area.

The renovation was long antici-pated. Six current tenants wanted to expand their presence in this region — they included some of the biggest names in luxury retail-ing: Gucci, Louis Vuitton, Dior, Coach, St. John and Brooks Brothers. Other upscale tenants wanted to lease space.

The renovation of the center's eastern section in 2003 involved 44,500 square feet, about one-fifth of the center's total space. Of that, about 3,500 square feet was new space. Renovation called for clos-ing the largest store, the 30,000-square-foot supermarket (an origi-nal tenant with a long-term lease), and various tenants with adjacent space whose leases would end simultaneously with that of the supermarket. Demolition of these spaces began immediately. Construction of the new section took 18 months.

The renovated area accommodated most of the retailers seeking more space and others. The owner engaged Peter Marino, a designer best known for his high-end fash-ion boutiques, to oversee architec-ture and design.

Photograph: © David Sundberg/Esto

An expanded Louis Vuitton store (above) is just one attraction at the renovated Americana Manhasset center on affluent Long Island, replacing dated exteriors (right).

Photograph: © David Sundberg/Esto

MAJOR TENANTS		
NAME	**TYPE**	**GLA (SQ. FT.)**
Ralph Lauren	Specialty retail	16,215
Brooks Brothers	Specialty retail	12,980
Tiffany & Co.	Specialty retail	6,925
Gucci	Specialty retail	5,776
St. John	Specialty retail	5,072
Louis Vuitton	Specialty retail	5,005
Giorgio Armani	Specialty retail	4,855

The old center (left) had a boxy exterior that did not serve the upscale shops therein.

New exteriors (below) feature whimsical sculpture, awnings, patterned sidewalks, enhanced landscaping and convenient parking.

The project's architectural distinction rests on its use of high-quality materials, reflecting the upscale ambience found inside the stores. Limestone facades, granite sidewalks and sleek lighting fixtures are the major building design components.

An exterior "fashion show" of color and texture comes from the relandscaped gardens, which lend a refreshing sensory experience as shoppers walk from store to store in the open air or to their conveniently parked vehicles. A rose garden was added, using large masses of plants to create a visual tapestry.

Photograph: © David Sundberg/Esto

Photograph: © David Sundberg/Esto

The enlarged space for the luxury retailers has reinforced the center's position as a high-end shopping destination. The quadrupling of space for Louis Vuitton, for example, has changed the nature of the store itself. Earlier, it offered mostly leather goods. Now, it is an emporium that has room to offer its ready-to-wear and fine-jewelry lines as well.

Photograph: © Peter Aaron/Esto

The addition of a trattoria has brought Americana Manhasset a nightlife it had previously lacked. The trattoria also owns a café nearby in the center, responding to upscale shoppers' requests for snacks and coffee.

Photograph: © David Sundberg/Esto

Photograph: © David Sundberg/Esto

Photograph: © David Sundberg/Esto

Photograph: © David Sundberg/Esto

Brooks Brothers and Bottega Veneta are among the high-end retailers that have benefited from their presence at the renovated Americana Manhasset center.

Photograph: © David Sundberg/Esto

The construction area, located at the eastern end of the property, was easily contained with a barricade. The construction team was housed in an onsite trailer. A guard was posted sentry at the gates day and night. Costumers were not inconvenienced and eagerly anticipated the opening of the new stores. An additional safety feature was added in renovation — an unused water pumping station on the property became a security booth for municipal police.

Marketing plans focused on the renovation. Advertisements, the center's Web site and other communications used a new tag line, "the evolution continues...." The owner initiated a shopper-recognition program. Media interviewed the owner, architect and landscape architect. Advertising dollars were doubled to include a weekly presence in the Styles section of the *New York Times*, reaching a national audience. A spring fashion book was added to the usual fall/holiday catalogs.

The renovation has enhanced the center's presence in the community, already strong from its community involvement. Its Champions for Charity® campaign during the holiday season, with 100 percent tenant participation, has generated over $2.3 million for charities in the past decade, generating good feelings for Americana Manhasset from its affluent neighbors.

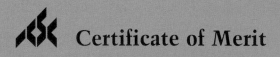 **Certificate of Merit**

Downtown Silver Spring

Silver Spring, Maryland, United States

Owner:
PFA (a joint venture between The Peterson Companies, Foulger-Pratt Companies and Argo Investments)
Silver Spring, Maryland, United States

Management Company:
The Peterson Companies
Fairfax, Virginia, United States

Architect:
RTKL Associates Inc.
Baltimore, Maryland, United States

Design and Production Architect:
Brown Craig Turner
Baltimore, Maryland, United States

Graphic Designer:
Brown Craig Turner
Baltimore, Maryland, United States

Lighting Designer:
Gary Gordon
New York, New York, United States

Landscape Architect:
Land Design
Alexandria, Virginia, United States

General Contractor:
Foulger-Pratt Construction
Rockville, Maryland, United States

Development Companies:
The Peterson Companies
Foulger-Pratt
Argo Investments
Silver Spring, Maryland, United States

Leasing Company:
The Peterson Companies
Silver Spring, Maryland, United States

Gross size of center:
- Before renovation/expansion
  35,000 sq. ft.
- After renovation/expansion
  265,000 sq. ft.

Current gross leasable area (small shop space, excluding anchors):
143,000 sq. ft.

Total acreage of site:
3.3 acres

Type of center:
Lifestyle

Physical description:
Open-air

Center's trade area:
Urban but not Central Business District

Population:
- Primary trading area
  224,119
- Secondary trading area
  564,021
- Annualized percentage of shoppers anticipated to be from outside trade area
  10%

Development schedule:
- Opening date
  1938
- Current renovation/expansion date
  Spring 2004

Parking spaces:
- Present number
  33
- 3,112 spaces on two county-owned parking decks

The central fountain at Downtown Silver Spring in suburban Maryland attracts youngsters and entertains visitors of all ages.

*D*owntown Silver Spring is a public/private joint venture between county government and three companies that has transformed a historic site that has been vacant for 10 years into a vibrant mixed-use venue.

Montgomery County, Maryland, had sought development to revitalize its core area. An advisory board agreed with the project development team that a bookstore, movie theater and restaurants were suitable tenants. Plans

called for a high-quality urban streetscape with pedestrian-scale furniture and lighting. A centrally located fountains acts as a giant "water cooler" bringing together diverse sectors of the community from early mornings through late evenings in spring, summer and fall.

Near the front door of Downtown Silver Spring is the historic art-deco Silver Spring Shopping Center, built in 1938, and Silver Theatre, both of which have been

An aerial view (top) of the project includes the historic Silver Theatre with its oval rear; an earlier aerial view lies right below. The center has revitalized the city core, encouraging alfresco dining. The old (immediately above) and new (below) facades epitomize the dramatic changes.

restored, renovated and expanded. The American Film Institute is now housed inside the theater, along with two smaller theaters. The developer used Historic Tax Credits for the AFI/Silver Theatre and Silver Spring Shopping Center renovations.

After the initial postwar period of suburban development, Silver Spring had begun to fall on hard times by the early 1970's. Retailers and companies, which had fueled Silver Spring's first growth, moved even farther away from downtown Washington, DC. The Silver Spring Shopping Center was closed in the late 1970's. Between 1989 and 1993, more than 300 companies left downtown Silver Spring, leaving 44 vacant buildings. Crime plagued the area. Only after the Montgomery County Council voted unanimously to add the Silver Spring Shopping Center to its historic preservation master plan would discussion begin on renovation.

By 1998, the PFA consortium — a joint venture between The Peterson Companies, Foulger-Pratt Companies and Argo

Investments — had agreed to redevelop the Silver Spring Shopping Center as part of an extensive new multiuse project to include two-level retail and 20-screen cinema buildings, dining options, green spaces, high-end retail, a 179-room, 10-story hotel and two new parking structures adjacent to the site. A future civic building is planned.

The Downtown Silver Spring project turned an abandoned crime-ridden area (above) into the vibrant, popular core of the community (above right).

Silver Plaza (left and below) is anchored by a stairway and a neon-accented elevator structure.

The project grew from extensive cooperation between public and private sectors. County government contributed $132 million toward acquisition and demolition. The development team created its plan, which would be reviewed by no fewer than 25 separate community associations.

One of the primary challenges for the project was overcoming a negative perception of an ethnically and economically mixed community with a high crime rate. By increasing the project's mass, Downtown Silver Spring became a destination unto itself. The owners budgeted $1 per square foot for security, present 24 hours daily.

Two major thoroughfares crisscross the site, but attractions that are spread out throughout the site draw customers into the various areas. A festival atmosphere pervades much of the site, with many gathering places lined by trees and accented by tall lighting fixtures. Neon lights accent store signs above table umbrellas. A brightly colored staircase and elevator structure serve to anchor the Silver Plaza area.

The restored Silver Spring Shopping Center now serves as a centerpiece in the new mixed-use complex. Pedestrian links aid flow across vehicular roads and major intersections. A pedestrian plaza, seating, sidewalks and signage complete the new Main Street look of Downtown Silver Spring.

MAJOR TENANTS		
NAME	**TYPE**	**GLA (SQ. FT.)**
Consolidated Theatres	Multiplex theater	97,000
Borders	Books and music	25,000

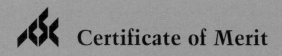

Certificate of Merit

The Galleria

Houston, Texas, United States

Owner and Management Company:
Simon Property Group
Indianapolis, Indiana, United States

Design Architect:
Cooper Carry, Inc.
Atlanta, Georgia, United States

Production Architect:
Cooper Carry, Inc.
Atlanta, Georgia, United States

Graphic Designer:
Kiku Obata & Company
St. Louis, Missouri, United States

Lighting Designer:
The Lighting Practice & Al Borden
Philadelphia, Pennsylvania, United States

Landscape Architect:
MESA Design Group
Dallas, Texas, United States

General Contractors:
Vratsinas Construction Company
Little Rock, Arkansas, United States
Turner Construction
Houston, Texas, United States

Development and Leasing Company:
Simon Property Group
Indianapolis, Indiana, United States

Gross size of center:
- Before renovation/expansion
  1,536,287 sq. ft.
- After renovation/expansion
  2,323,568 sq. ft.

Current gross leasable area (small shop space, excluding anchors):
996,502 sq. ft.

Total acreage of site:
36.4 acres

Type of center:
Superregional center

Physical description:
Three-level enclosed mall

Center's trade area:
Urban Central Business District

Population:
- Primary trading area
  664,028
- Secondary trading area
  703,745
- Annualized percentage of shoppers anticipated to be from outside trade area
  30%

Development schedule:
- Opening date
  1970
- Current renovation/expansion date
  Oct. 2002 (renovation)
  March 2003 (expansion)

Parking spaces:
- 12,995 for the entire mixed-use project
- Number added in renovation/expansion
  2,741

An aerial view shows The Galleria in downtown Houston. A renovated area reopened about five months before a large-scale expansion. The clerestory ceiling (upper right) in the expansion area offers natural light.

The Galleria in downtown Houston, Texas, undertook both a renovation and expansion soon after completing its third decade as one of the area's largest shopping destinations. The region had grown dramatically since The Galleria's opening in 1970. The mall is a destination unto itself, hosting over 17 million people each year.

The renovation updated the center's interior look. The expansion continued the renovation's new look and allowed growing tenants to occupy more space.

Over 818,000 square feet of space was renovated. A large wood and glass elevator was added near the east end of the well-known skating rink. Floors previously covered with carpet and tile now show nine types of marble from seven countries, creating an international style. Ceilings once made of acoustic tile were replaced by lighter-colored drywall that better articulates the building's struc-

Retailers (above) were able to grow into new space, thanks to the expansion project. Water falls 50 feet from a "chandelier" (right), offering visual entertainment.

An interior view of the new expansion area concourse (below) and the exterior of the new six-level parking deck (bottom) show elements of modern design.

MAJOR TENANTS		
NAME	**TYPE**	**GLA (SQ. FT.)**
Foley's	Department store	250,000
Macy's	Department store	232,000
Nordstrom	Department store	218,000
Neiman Marcus	Department store	200,000
Saks Fifth Avenue	Department store	185,500
University Club	Health club	105,000

ture, creating a dynamic rhythm to the space.

Custom light fixtures also support the modern style achieved through renovation. The second and third floors now contain cantilevered balconies overlooking the ice rink. Shoppers can now take a break by relaxing in soft leather sofas and chairs throughout the mall, which are particularly welcomed by those watching the skaters. Transparent-glass and stainless-steel guardrails replaced aluminum-picket railings on the

second and third floors. Finally, the existing 4,500-square-foot barrel skylight over the ice rink, previously glazed with brown acrylic, has been redone with high-performance glass. The renovated section opened its doors in October 2002.

The expansion opened five months later. The two-level structure, built over a two-level parking garage containing about 800 parking spaces, contains small shops and department store anchors Nordstrom and Foley's.

The 700-foot expansion concourse is in a slightly curved form that creates interesting sight lines within the corridor. A continuous clerestory punctuates the concourse with skylights, allowing more natural light to reach the lower levels. Beyond the two-level garage below the mall, customers are also served by the 2,800 parking spaces in a new six-level parking deck.

The Galleria's new section used the same materials and, when possible, the same details as the mall's renovated area. In addition, a 20-foot-wide falling-water feature provides entertainment at the court outside the new Foley's department store. The cylindrical column of water falls 50 feet from a stainless-steel "water chandelier" in a computerized, choreographed pattern.

The Galleria was open during both renovation and expansion. Renovation work was done mostly after business hours in deference to pedestrian congestion and shopper safety. Pedestrians were isolated from active construction. Expansion took place in a confined construction area. Neither renovation nor expansion had meaningful impact on sales during the construction period.

Renovation and expansion proved appealing to tenants. The smaller leasable area preexpansion had been 83% occupied. Tenant occu-

pancy rate rose to 92% postexpansion.

The landmark Houston mall is now reclad in classic modern style. Onyx and exotic woods are among the high-end finishing materials from around the world, essential to creating a truly world-class shopping experience at The Galleria.

Dark and dreary views of the old Galleria (left column, above) gave way to the lighter colors and natural light of the mall's new look (right column). In the renovated section of The Galleria, hungry or weary shoppers find comfort at the updated food court (bottom left) or in soft seating areas (bottom right).

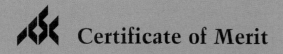

Shopping Center Iguatemi Fortaleza

Fortaleza, Ceará, Brazil

Owners:

Jereissati Centros Comerciais
Fortaleza, Ceará, Brazil

Petros Fundacão Petrobrás de Seguridade Social
Rio de Janeiro, Rio de Janeiro, Brazil

Management Company:
Shopping Centers Iguatemi
Fortaleza, Ceará, Brazil

Design Architects:
ID8
Baltimore, Maryland, United States

RTKL Associates Inc.
Dallas, Texas, United States

Production Architects:
Gerardo Jereissati, Paulo Cezar Arraes, Raimundo Calixto de Melo
Fortaleza, Ceará, Brazil

Graphic Designer:
Mário Roque
Fortaleza, Ceará, Brazil

Lighting Designer:
T. Kondos Associates
New York, New York, United States

General Contractor:
Gerardo Jereissati
Fortaleza, Ceará, Brazil

Development and Leasing Company:
Jereissati Centros Comerciais
Fortaleza, Ceará, Brazil

Gross size of center:
- Before renovation/expansion
  467,340 sq. ft.
- After renovation/expansion
  594,170 sq. ft.

Current gross leasable area (small shop space, excluding anchors):
257,800 sq. ft.

Total acreage of site:
35.8 acres

Type of center:
Regional

Physical description:
Enclosed mall

Center's trade area:
Urban but not Central Business District

Population:
- Primary trading area
  17,000
- Secondary trading area
  93,000
- Annualized percentage of shoppers anticipated to be from outside trade area
  5%

Development schedule:
- Opening date
  April 1982
- Current expansion date
  July 2003

Parking spaces:
- Present number
  3,900
- Number added in renovation/expansion
  500

Shopping Center Iguatemi Fortaleza on Brazil's northeast shore serves Fortaleza, the fifth largest city in the nation. Per capita income of its two million residents is among the lowest in Brazil.

When the center opened in 1982, the shopping center concept was new in the State of Ceará. The center had about 100 stores, four anchors, two movie theaters and a small food court. Its success changed the habits of residents and store owners. Its first expansion was in 1992, adding another 100 stores and three movie theaters. The food court was expanded to seat 600.

By the late 1990's, vacancy was at zero and hopeful retailers began looking for locations in nearby community centers. Seeing this tendency grow, Iguatemi Fortaleza's owners decided to expand the center once more.

Other factors entered into play. Fortaleza did not have stadium-seating movie theaters. Shoppers also wanted a large sporting goods store and parking lots that were sheltered from the Brazilian heat and closer to the stores. In planning for the renovation and expansion, the developers and designers incorporated those needs and also built in an entertainment option for the community.

Throughout the years, shoppers had come to expect innovation from Iguatemi Fortaleza. In 1982, they had never before seen a

Imaginative sculpture and symbols of the sea beckon to shoppers approaching the exterior of Shopping Center Iguatemi Fortaleza.

MAJOR TENANTS		
NAME	TYPE	GLA (SQ. FT.)
EXTRA	Supermarket	130,000
UCI-Ribeiro	Multiscreen theater	60,000
Riachuelo	Department store	57,000
Lojas Americanas	Department store	42,000
C&A	Department store	28,000

Aerial views of the earlier building (top) and the expanded center (above) show, at lower right, where the expansion replaced a parking lot.

In the main court (below), the main entrance (lower right) and storefronts visibility and visual excitement get high design priority.

slightly curved roof with the spatial design that they found at this center. In the 1992 expansion, designers imported multicolored glass for the building's skylights — as a result, the light in the center changed throughout the day.

The expansion established Iguatemi Fortaleza as the only regional mall in the State of Ceará to have a tenant mix that included a supermarket, department stores and other chains, food courts, multiplex movie theaters and a wide range of small shops and services.

The expansion is on three levels articulated around a central square. Designers sought to create a playful, social atmosphere, mix-

ing elements from the local culture with modern materials and technologies. Design within Iguatemi Fortaleza evokes the relationship of its people with the ocean, using symbols such as the raft, fish, ocean waves, palm trees and flowers. Each symbol was reinterpreted and stylized. The overall motif is replicated in the project's most important elements

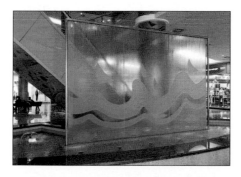

— the facade, the floor and the fountains.

The new sporting goods store is on the main floor. One flight up from the main floor are a restaurant and the ticket booths for the cinema. The 12 theaters are on the top floor. The lower two floors have direct access to the parking lot.

The main floor also holds the Grand Awning with its high ceiling supported by a single column of tensioned steel. Above this support is a mirrored glass ceiling, offering the image of a great kaleidoscope. Shoppers walking through this area stop at the fountain, with water gliding over a sculpted glass wall with bas-

reliefs of marine motifs. The floor is made of granite of varying colors and shapes, extracted from local quarries. Internal columns are coated with shriveled stainless steel, modeled on palm tree trunks. Nearby bulkheads contain inscriptions in many languages, evoking concepts of liberty, love and peace.

All flow elements — escalators, stairs and the panoramic elevator — lead to the main attraction, the central square. This space is meant for lounging. Benches are aligned with the medallion and are turned toward a large projection screen. A large medallion is in the granite floor, containing the ocean and land symbols found throughout the center. Swarovski crystals on the ceiling of the central square produce a skylike effect with the constellations of the zodiac.

The project's success is told in the fact that vacancies remain below one percent and both shopper volume and sales increased despite a nationwide economic recession at the time of the expansion's opening. Shopping Center Iguatemi Fortaleza continues to be the premier retail destination in its region.

*(Left, from top:)
Inside, a huge projection screen entertains shoppers at the central square. The main floor holds ticket booths for the second-level movie theaters. Recessed lighting reflects pinpoints on a mall floor. A glass fountain and a floor medallion remind shoppers of the region's historic ties to land and sea.*

The exterior of the center (top right) shows several of the land and sea symbols that enhance the design of Shopping Center Iguatemi Fortaleza.

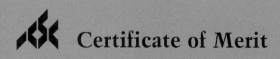

The Woodlands Mall

The Woodlands, Texas, United States

Owner and Management Company:
General Growth Properties, Inc.
Chicago, Illinois, United States

Design and Production Architect:
RTKL Associates Inc.
Dallas, Texas, United States

Graphic Designer:
RTKL Associates Inc.
Los Angeles, California, United States

Lighting Designer:
T. Kondos Associates
New York, New York, United States

Landscape Architect:
MESA Design Group
Dallas, Texas, United States

General Contractor:
BBC
Little Rock, Arkansas, United States

Development and Leasing Companies:
General Growth Properties, Inc.
Chicago, Illinois, United States

Gross size of center:
- Before renovation/expansion
  1,175,460
- After renovation/expansion
  1,352,543

Current gross leasable area (small shop space, excluding anchors):
526,028 sq. ft.

Total acreage of site:
31 acres

Type of center:
Superregional lifestyle/fashion

Physical description:
Two-level open-air and enclosed mall

Center's trade area:
Suburban

Population:
- Primary trading area
  55,700
- Secondary trading area
  293,700
- Annualized percentage of shoppers anticipated to be from outside trade area
  5%

Development schedule:
- Opening date
  1994
- Current expansion date
  May 18, 2004

Parking spaces:
- Present number
  5,900
- None added in renovation/expansion

*T*he expansion of the 10-year-old Woodlands Mall brought an outdoor retail/entertainment component to an enclosed retail center. As part of a master plan for a mixed-use urban center of over 100 acres — the idea of the project was to create an outdoor, urban-style town center in a suburban area — the project created a lifestyle-focused streetscape to expand the existing center and link it to the new town center.

Before expansion, The Woodlands Mall was a fully leased successful superregional mall. Despite declining sales at many other malls nationwide, The Woodlands Mall had enjoyed steady growth through the years. In 2001, a master plan for a new urban district in the area was announced. Along with market demand for high-end retail and continuing evidence of the success of streetscape environments, the stage was set for the open-air expansion of the enclosed Woodlands Mall on a site that previously held a parking field.

Now, the entry to the mall is framed by the open-air expansion, which also functions as the turning point in the town's waterway system. A water taxi is available. A quadrant of four restaurants and outdoor dining terraces center on the waterway. The streetscape is enhanced by the presence of boat landings, outdoor dining porches, fountains and benches.

On one side, vehicular tenant entrances can easily access parking spaces. Through-unit configu-

The Woodlands Mall expansion focused on a waterway in the heart of the site, a dramatic feature in architect's rendering (below) or in reality (above).

Photograph: Courtesy of RTKL Associates Inc.

Photograph: Courtesy of RTKL Associates Inc.

MAJOR TENANTS		
NAME	TYPE	GLA (SQ. FT.)
Barnes & Noble	Bookstore	18,350
Pottery Barn	Specialty	13,383
The Cheesecake Factory	Food	12,000
Urban Outfitters	Clothing	11,008
Anthropologie	Clothing	8,792

(At far left, from top:) The former Woodlands Mall entrance, complemented by the new expansion. Metallic awnings and complementary signage bring shoppers into stores. A walkable streetscape brings a hometown feel to shopping. Tenant storefronts (bottom left) were blended into the overall design concept.

Extensive landscaping, streetlamps and patterned paving (below) are among the consistent design elements used at The Woodlands Mall expansion.

rations link surface parking lots to the linear, pedestrian-oriented streetscape. A cohesive design scheme balances tenant branding and materials with unifying elements.

The through-unit structure presented a unique design challenge. Typically, such configurations present a sales hindrance. At The Woodlands Mall, however, designers addressed this issue by creating unified, aesthetically pleasing facades at both vehicular and pedestrian tenant entrances. Designers were careful to maintain the center's design concept despite the distinctive nature and branding of individual tenants. High-quality materials and abundant landscaping were used in the front and back of tenant facades. Alongside tenant-specific materials, designers included a series of green metal overhangs that serve as a unifying element. The overhangs complement glass windows, metal detailing and innovative lighting features that contribute to a cohesive visual environment.

The owner and new and existing retail and entertainment venues near the expansion area took steps to maintain normal operations during construction. For example, The Cheesecake Factory, one of the first shops completed in the expansion, had the developer build a tunnel that linked the restaurant into the existing enclosed mall while other construction continued.

Intrinsic to the expansion's success was the use of atypical anchors such as Barnes & Noble. With them, the expanded area offers a twist on the usual mixed-use development. The leasing plan targeted a range of markets, from the young hipsters who would be attracted to stores like Urban Outfitters to upper-income homeowners who sought out Williams-Sonoma and Pottery Barn.

The expansion has had a dramatic effect on the center. Both rents and sales doubled postexpansion — evidence that providing a new type of shopping environment at an established destination can have a positive impact overall.

Atypical anchors, entertainment venues and food outlets add up to retail success at The Woodlands Mall.

Congratulations!
2005 ICSC European Awards Recipients and Finalists

Every year since 1975 ICSC Europe recognise excellence in new and refurbished and extended projects. From 29 countries across Western, Eastern & Central Europe, Scandinavia, Turkey, The Baltic States, Ukraine and Russia. From a shortlist of Finalists, outstanding schemes are selected as Award winners by a jury of international specialists. Commendations may also be given to select Finalists to recognise particular achievements or features of special interest.

A new honour named "ReStore" has been introduced for the first time this year to recognise specific urban regeneration work.

2005 Awards: New Projects

Bullring
Birmingham, UK

Stary Browar
Poznan, Poland

Kamp Promenade
Osnabrück, Germany

2005 Commendations: New Projects

Estaçao Viana
Viana do Castelo, Portugal

Les Grand Prés
Mons, Belgium

Klanderij
Enschede, The Netherlands

2005 Refurbishments

Olympia Einkaufz.
Munich, Germany

2005 ReStore

Klanderij
Enschede, Netherlands

Other 2005 Finalists

Berceo, Logroño, Spain
Bruno Gotgtsbacken, Stockholm, Sweden
Castlepoint, Bournemouth, United Kingdom
Centro Meridiana, Casalecchio di Reno, Italy
El Boulevard, Vitoria, Spain
Olympia Olomouc, Olomouc, Czech Republic
Parque Atlántico, Ponta Delgada, Azores, Portugal
Riem Arcaden, Munich, Germany
Ski Storsenter, Ski, Norway